THESE ARE THE DAYS OF MY LIFE

Endorsements

What a gift it would be if you or I could find a handbook with all the answers to overcoming all of life's challenges. Deb Haggerty has come very close to creating just that! Within these pages, you'll discover the joy of laughing before whining, praying before crying, loving before blaming and embracing before ignoring. Her gift of storytelling combined with her penchant for creative writing will keep you turning page after page, nonstop. You will find yourself greeting life's challenges with renewed hope and enhanced happiness.

—**Glenna Salsbury**, Hall of Fame Professional Speaker, author of *The Art of the Fresh Start.*

These are the Days of My Life is a treasured collection of uplifting and personal stories, but what makes this collection different from many others is Deb Haggerty's openness and vulnerability in how she shares them with us. Her stories remind me of Aesop as they not only inspire, but leave us with transforming life coaching. Once you start reading, you won't want to put this book down.

—**Wayne Hastings**, President of the Wayne Hastings Co., LLC and author of *The Way Back From Loss: Reassembling the Pieces of a Broken Life.*

These Are The Days Of My Life did not take long to read and left me wanting to go back and read it again. Deb Haggerty has a way of touching the heart with her words as she replayed the joys and struggles of life while highlighting God's faithfulness on the journey.

I laughed and I cried and at the end of the book I found myself thanking God for His work in Deb's life. Then I praised Him for His work in my own. What a special book!

—**Shelley Pierce**, award-winning author of the *Crumberry Chronicles* and *Sweet Moments: Insight and Encouragement for the Pastor's Wife.*

These Are the Days of My Life is a resourceful book offering Deb Haggerty's story, wisdom about life struggles, and encouragement for success in publishing and business. As you read, you'll be grateful for her sense of humor and honest sharing because her words will boost your positive perspective.

—**Kathy Collard Miller and Larry Miller**, speakers and author of multiple books including *God's Intriguing Questions: 100 Devotionals Revealing God's Qualities and Our Motives.*

These Are the Days of My Life is an honest blend of Deb's personal and business life. While she lets us into the struggles of her breast cancer journey and losing a son, she also shows us the humor and joy in her life. The business essays are relevant to all of us and provide excellent insights about networking and communication we may not have known before. You'll relish this engaging read through one woman's busy world.

—**Georgia Shaffer**, Professional Certified Coach, PA Licensed Psychologist, and author of five books, including *Taking Out Your Emotional Trash.*

Deb Haggerty's faith and spiritual growth shines through every page of her life experiences in *These Are the Days of My Life*. Grow with her as she shares the peaks and valleys of her life journey with God.

—**DiAnn Mills**, award-winning author of *Fatal Strike* (Tyndale, 9-19), DiAnnMills.com.

These Are the Days of My Life is a humorous and insightful look into the life of a talented woman who has learned to step out of her comfort zone in order to positively touch the lives of others. She shares valuable information and advice for those who wish to find out more about themselves or who wish to succeed in the publishing industry.

—**Derinda Babcock**, author of the *Destiny Trilogy* and *Colorado Treasure*.

A memoir full of bite-size stories containing lessons Deb Haggerty learned from life with family, friends, and in the workplace. If you enjoy reading memoirs, there's much to draw from in *These Are the Days of My Life*.

Her stories containing life lessons learned provide experiences we can all draw from, whether we're dealing with family, friends, life's tragedies, or life on the job.

—**H. L. Wegley,** author of *Switched, Virtuality,* and other up-to-the-moment suspense thrillers.

Deb Haggerty's book, *These are the Days of My Life*, is powerful and offers hope and encouragement to those who are dealing with the everyday trials of life. By sharing her own personal triumphs and tragedies, struggles and successes, she shares how you can persevere in life. She also shows how even the darkest experiences in life can lead to a bright tomorrow.

I wholeheartedly recommend this book because it is an encouraging, emotional, and exciting read.

—Dell R. Hyssong Jr., author, *Joy for the Journey* and *Mikayla's Heart*, baritone and trumpet for The Hyssongs, an award-winning gospel music trio.

Part memoir. Part devotional. A little bit poetry. Some sorrow. Lots of humor. Mostly *These Are the Days of My Life* is Deb Haggerty. I heard her voice telling me the stories that have made up her life. Do you want to be encouraged, feel supported, have a laugh, get to know Deb? This is the book that will do all of that.

—Susan K. Stewart, author, Practical Inspirations Editing

THESE ARE THE DAYS OF MY LIFE

Deb Haggerty

PUBLISHING THE POSITIVE

ELK LAKE PUBLISHING INC
Plymouth, Massachusetts

Cover and Interior Design: Derinda Babcock

Editor: Cristel Phelps

LIBRARY CATALOGING DATA

Names: Haggerty, Deb (Deb Haggerty)

These Are the Days of My Life / Deb Haggerty

152 p. 23cm × 15cm (9in × 6 in.)

Description: PUBLISHED BY: Elk Lake Publishing, Inc., 35 Dogwood Drive, Plymouth, MA 02360, 2019

Identifiers: ISBN-13: | 978-1-951080-95-2 (trade paperback)

| 978-1-951080-53-2 (POD) | 978-1-951080-54-9 (e-book)

Key Words: Breast Cancer, Death of Child, Stepparenting, Marriage, Writing, Business, Inspirational

LCCN: 2019952437 Nonfiction

DEDICATION

To my husband, Roy.

Honey, we've been through so much together, but you still make me laugh every day and treasure life. I value your wisdom, your support, and most of all your love.

TABLE OF CONTENTS

THESE ARE THE DAYS OF MY LIFE i

Endorsements ii

Copyright Notice. vi

Dedication. ix

Acknowledgments xiii

Introduction 1

Step Out of Your Comfort Zone 7

Me Too 11

Sleep 15

Hooked, Netted, and Set Free 17

Skee Ball, Pizza Fights, and Fun! 23

Light That Fire! 25

Oh, I Get It! 27

RummiKub Summer 31

Jimmy's Bike 33

Even Atlanta 37

Aloha, Hawaii 39

Relationships Are Everything. 41

Business Suits to Bunny Slippers 45

No Longer the Ugly Stepmother 49

The Spirit of Santa Claus 55

To Dad 57

Instant Friends, Sisters for Life. 59

Coincidences? Not a Chance!. 61

Distress Signal 65

And the Comfort Overflows 67

Checkerboard Hair 69

A Special Kind of Encouragement 73

Through Good Times and Bad. 75

Music of the Tube 77

Six Feet Tall—And Bald. 79

Reincarnation or Resurrection? 83

I Will Fear No Evil. 85

A Godly Woman's Influence. 87

God Is in Control 89

My Mother's Hands. 91

Mom 93

Starting Over—AGAIN! 95

Conclusion 99

About the Author. 101

KEYS TO SUCCESSFUL WRITING. 103

Pet Peeves. 105

The ART of Exceptional Editing 107

Writing, Teaching, Acquiring. 111

Choose Your Publisher with Care. 113

Conference Season Is Upon Us 117

People Are Important! 121

Communication—Our Most Important Asset. 123

ACKNOWLEDGMENTS

No book is born without the efforts of many people over a long period of time. This book is comprised of stories I wrote over thirty-some years for other people's books or for magazines. I thank all the many people who published my stories and articles all those years.

These Are the Days of My Life would still not have been birthed had not Angie Breidenbach encouraged me to put the stories together and publish them.

Derinda Babcock taught me InDesign and how to format books. She also designed the wonderful cover. I have been blessed with her talents as an author, graphic designer, and book formatter for several years and am so grateful.

Cristel Phelps edited for me and caught those picky little things so easily missed. The book is better for her efforts.

Pam Burks, a long time friend from the National Speakers Association, caught all the errors the rest of us missed.

My wonderful husband, Roy, was my beta reader and gave me great suggestions and much encouragement during the process. Living with him and James and Jill gave me much of my material. Thanks, guys!

Most of all, I thank my Savior and Lord, Jesus Christ, for giving me this ministry and all the blessings we enjoy. I would be nothing without him.

INTRODUCTION

When I was growing up, my mom worked during the day at my parents' business, but she always came home at lunchtime to watch her soap opera, *Days of Our Lives*. During summer vacations, I watched along with her.

But kids grow up and go out on their own, as did I. I went through ups and downs and lived my own soap opera. In 1983, I married the love of my life, Roy, and acquired two children, Jill and James. We've lived our soap opera as well, with tragedy and triumph. We've moved several times—from New Jersey to Pennsylvania to Florida to Massachusetts. My mom, Shirley Ogle, came to live with us in Orlando and then Plymouth. We've had a variety of dogs—first Max, then Coco, then Coki.

Now, we live on beautiful Boot Pond outside Plymouth, Massachusetts. Coki the Dog is still with us, but Dad, Mom, and James have gone to be with the Lord. Our daughter, Jill, is the mom of our handsome grandson, William, and a successful businesswoman in her own right.

I've often thought how our lives seem to be a soap opera, with ups and downs, sad and happy times, good and bad. Looking back now from my seventies, I'm amused at what I thought and lived through back then. You may be entertained as well as you read some of the adventures in *These Are the Days of My Life*.

Count it all joy, my brothers, when you meet trials of various kinds, for you know that the testing of your faith produces steadfastness. And let steadfastness have its full effect, that you may be perfect and complete, lacking in nothing. (James 1:2-4, ESV)

The Adventures of My Life

Step Out of Your Comfort Zone

Once upon a time, I was very, very shy. Naturally tall, I had a perception of myself as overweight as well, and to top it off, I was smart. Tall, fat, smart girls don't date much. I was self-conscious and awkward and had low self esteem. Oh, I had some friends, and we did many enjoyable things together, but I always felt out of place.

When I went to college, I picked a school where no one else from my hometown was going. I hoped I would be able to make a fresh start and leave the "old" me behind. But she followed me—I was still oh so shy. I wanted to break out of my shell and be one of the popular people, but I just couldn't do it.

I was so shy I would cut class if I thought I was going to be late, because I couldn't stand the thought of people looking at me when I walked in. If a stranger talked to me, I blushed. I had a very hard time making eye contact. The only time I was comfortable was when I was being someone else.

In high school, I had discovered debate and declamation and drama. Excelling at these activities allowed me to receive approbation for what I was doing, even though I didn't feel approval for myself as a person. So I got involved in similar activities in college. All I wanted, though, was to be one of the gang, to date, to be thought of as petite (in my dreams), and bouncy and cute—things that were out of the realm of possibility physically or in actions.

Once, when I was at a dance, occupying my normal wallflower position at the side of the room, I noticed another girl in a similar position. The thought occurred to me: What if I go talk to her? The worst thing that can happen is she might refuse to talk to me. I did just that. I went over and introduced myself, we became friends, and that incident started my road toward victory over shyness.

I realized many people are really shy under their calm exterior, and they might welcome someone else breaking the ice and talking to them. I realized if they spurned my attempt at conversation, they had lost the opportunity to make a new acquaintance. From that realization came my practice of talking to and with almost anybody. I have made the best friends and had some of my most wonderful experiences since "talking to strangers" became my habit.

I began to observe the people around me whom I viewed as having the ability to make friends. One of the best was my dad. He never knew a stranger; they were just friends he hadn't yet met. He didn't view people as superiors or inferiors; they were just "folks." The motto at his place of business was "Howard Wants to See You!" and his customers always felt exactly that way.

After learning to overcome my shyness, acquiring friends and resources became a way of life for me. Knowing who to call for information or to find out how to do something was as important as knowing it myself or having the actual information at my fingertips.

I became a professional speaker. The "escapes" I used in high school and college became my profession. I am told by many people they have seen few others who have my ability to speak to an audience of any size and make each member feel as if they are being spoken to personally and individually. I am also told my audiences feel as if they are a part of my life and that they can become "new best friends" with me if they so desire.

Knowing I am a person of value and worth has made all the difference in my professional and private life. Being "brave" enough to talk with people has brought me some of the most rewarding times. A few years ago, when I was ill, I received email notes from many people I had met on various occasions. They told me my smile at them or the brief conversations we had engaged in or the introductions I had made for them had benefited them greatly and made lasting impressions on them.

I am still shy, although most of the people I know would never believe it. However, I operate out of my comfort zone on a daily basis, because the benefits far outweigh the risks. Not only do I make new friends and establish new relationships, but those people I meet also find others who become friends. By being an example, I have given others the courage to reach out and meet new people and make new friends.

My passion for speaking and writing exists to connect others through positive strategies in communication and networking. I now teach people how to build relationships with others and to network for positive connections.

Me Too

"Deb, I have wonderful news for you! Headquarters has noticed your work, and you're being promoted to company headquarters."

"Ooh, that's great! Where am I going to be working?"

"You're going to be reporting to Sam Thomas* in Marketing Administration."

"Ooh, no! Isn't there anyone else I could be assigned to?"

"No, I'm sorry. Sam Thomas requested you when he heard you were available. What you need to do is accept the position, do an excellent job, and later, if a position becomes available, you can request a transfer."

I was disappointed at the position and the boss I was to report to as stories of Sam Thomas and his shenanigans had made the rounds. But turning down the promotion wasn't an option. And to tell the truth, sexual harassment was the order of the day in many of our offices. Women weren't common in the positions or offices where I worked at that time.

So, I accepted the position and relocated to company headquarters. I sold my home and purchased another, so the transfer took some time.

Day one on my new job, I was arranging my desk when my boss appeared in the door of his office.

(*Not his real name)

"Deb, come into my office, please?"

"Coming."

"Close the door on your way in."

"Oh, Mr. Thomas. I'm expecting a call—do you mind if I leave the door open a bit?"

"Okay. Sit here, and we'll go through your responsibilities."

As he began to tell me what I would be doing, he leaned way back in his chair and began rubbing his zipper area, all the while talking and smirking at the same time.

"Mr. Thomas," I said. "What you are doing is very offensive to me. Let's start this relationship off on an equal, respecting-each-other basis. I won't sue you for sexual harassment if you stop that behavior, and you won't sue me for insubordination if I refuse to put up with this."

Quite taken aback, Sam sat up straight in his chair and continued his briefing in a professional manner. From that day on, he showed me nothing but respect. We became quite good friends and protected each other when difficulties arose for our department. Sam wasn't adept politically and continually struggled for resources for his department and his people. I took on more and more responsibilities to help smooth the way for him. Early in my career, I'd learned the best way to get promoted and to get along with my bosses was to make them look good.

When the time came for Sam to retire, he ensured my placement in the best district in our division. He later wrote me a letter telling me he knew that without me, he would have been let go before he came to retirement age. Sam's gone now, but the memory of the scene in his office that day stayed with me throughout my career.

As I progressed up the ranks in the corporation, I made sure I had an understanding with my male bosses of what was and wasn't acceptable behavior—from both viewpoints. I did the same thing with my subordinates. As a result, camaraderie was great in our organizations and respect instead of harassment ran rampant. A pat on the shoulder was accepted as a sign of approval, not a come on. Joking was clean and no longer filled with sexual overtones.

I learned a lot through that experience. I learned I did not have to accept sexual innuendo or advances from anyone. I learned firmness with respect gained respect. I learned respect could be given to the position even when not earned by the individual. I learned taking the high road always brought benefits. I learned putting advances down with a smile or a joke brought respect not recrimination.

On one occasion, I was to make a presentation to the executive committee. I dressed in my best suit to make that all-important first good impression. One of the VPs on his way in commented, "I see you have your power suit on today, Deb. Are you trying to intimidate us?"

I laughed and replied, "Oh, no. I don't have to wear a power suit to intimidate you!" He took the retort with good humor, realizing his comment wasn't appropriate (and neither was mine), but we were able to get past the comments with humor and respect.

At another event, I was asked by a high-powered attorney in attendance, "Are you sure you can handle all us sharks in the audience?"

My retort was, "I've always found it much more fun to swim with sharks than guppies." His friends laughed at the comeback because the man was known for his intimidation techniques. Again, I gained respect when I took no offense.

15

Harassment of all types is many times a two-way street. Guys give signals they'd like you to approach them; gals give signals they're approachable. Is either behavior proper? No. The "Me Too" movement made coming forward in cases of harassment by either males or females acceptable and universally condemns harassment of all kinds. I'm glad I learned how to handle those situations early in my career and could stop them before they began.

SLEEP

I lie here in my bed fighting sleep.
Why do I force my eyes to stay open
Even when tear-filled yawns fill my face?
I am lonely. Perhaps that is why.
I yearn for companionship, a cuddle, a voice—
Sleepy, mumbled "I love yous."
But that was yesterday, many yesterdays ago.
Now, I am alone, here in my bed.

Hooked, Netted, and Set Free

Minnesota is the land of ten thousand lakes (and twenty thousand potholes) with a fish in every one if you listen to the fishermen. It's also a land of churches. I'd grown up going to church, but I was first "hooked" when I was eighteen.

I'd been attending a small congregational church, but I had questions. I watched the people who came each week. Like all churches, there were those who came to be seen and show people they were religious. Then there were those who came and seemed to have a sense of joy and contentment. I wondered why they were that way as many of them were very poor and had almost nothing. I wanted the joy they had and wondered what the source of that joy was. I assumed religion, so as a studious gal, I researched religion—from the theology of that church to the Eastern religions—and I found no answers, just more questions.

The summer of my senior year in high school, a girlfriend and I started attending a church in a town not too far from the lake cottage we stayed in summers. She enticed me to go with her by telling me the new associate pastor would be able to answer all my questions.

Phil did answer all those pesky theological questions, but then he asked, "Deb, do you know Jesus?"

"Of course I know Jesus. Everybody does. You know, Christmas, Easter, all that stuff."

"No, I mean do you know him as a person. Is he someone you can talk to? Cry with? Take walks with? Share your problems with? Do you know him like that?"

"Well, no. Not that way."

"Would you like to?"

"Yes, oh yes, I would."

Phil said, "Deb, the Bible teaches us all people have sinned and fall short of the glory of God—what God expects of them. And the punishment for sin is death—eternal separation from God. But the free gift of God is eternal life through Christ Jesus if we turn away from our sins and believe in him.

"Deb, do you understand? Do you want to become his?"

"Yes, please."

That was the day Jesus became real to me. I was securely hooked.

What happens when a fish is hooked? It swims up to the boat and jumps in, right? No, it struggles to get away from the hook. So did I. I swam away for years.

On the outside, I was a responsible adult, who had a career, friends, and went to church on Sundays. On the inside, I was anything but. Oh, I did all the right things, but I was so insecure. I "looked for love in all the wrong places."

My life at night was drinking, smoking (only cigarettes—I wouldn't do drugs of any kind), and going from one relationship to another. I kept seeking something that would make me feel good about myself. But I found nothing. I married and divorced—twice.

During the day, I was pursuing my career. I received several promotions and not only moved up in level, but up the coast from city to city. When I was thirty-something, I was promoted to my dream job—I was now in the top seven percent of managers in the largest corporation (at that time) in the world. I was in heaven!

And then reality set in. That, too, was empty. What now? Did I keep striving for higher levels, more responsibility, more moves? Was that all there was to life?

My double life continued—responsible adult during the day, party girl at night.

And then, I met the man who would become my forever husband. I was so confident I'd found the perfect guy for me—finally. We found a house; we built a life together. But we argued—about his kids, about our goals, about finances, about sex. Far from the perfection I'd envisioned.

During this time, we found a church to attend. One Sunday, I heard the Lord say very strongly, "Come back to me." I felt enveloped in love and so wanted to agree. The feeling and voice were so strong I looked around to see if anyone else had heard.

But I thought about my past life. "Oh no, Lord. You can't still want me. I've done too many things against your will. I'm too bad."

Then the verse popped into my head: "All that the Father gives to me will come to me, and the one who comes to me I will certainly not cast out" (John 6:37 NASB). At that moment, I was reeled in and netted. I realized all the time I was struggling, I was still connected to his line.

Paraphrasing Micah 7:10, "The Lord takes our sins, bundles them up, then casts them into the deepest sea and posts a sign that says, 'No fishing!'"

I finally accepted God had forgiven even me. But I couldn't forgive myself. The things I'd done kept coming to my mind over and over. Then a Corrie ten Boom quote came to mind.

"Forgiveness is setting the prisoner free, only to find out that the prisoner was me." I concentrated on believing I was free. The past was past, and I could live for today and tomorrow. He catches us to free us from this world and our past sins and life, "So if the Son sets you free, you will be free indeed" (John 8:36 NIV).

The wonder of all this was I was no longer living a double life. My daytime and nighttime selves had merged. I learned to curb my acerbic tongue (most of the time). I learned to respect and love my husband and what he was trying to do for us. I learned fulfillment comes from within. I learned my happiness and joy depended on me.

You're thinking, "Oh, she's going to tell us she has a perfect life now." No, I'm not. Bad things happen to good people all the time. Although my husband's job made us financially secure, and we had a beautiful home and all the trappings of success, we still experienced life.

Over a fourteen-year span, we lost both our dads, both our moms, and our son was killed in a freak automobile accident. I was diagnosed with breast cancer and endured a dual mastectomy and chemo. My speaking career came to a halt when I strongly felt I needed to stay at home to care for my mother who'd come to live with us.

From 1999 to now, our life has turned topsy-turvy. The losses we experienced have affected us deeply. My husband retired. We moved again—to the house his mom had left him and where he'd spent summers growing up. We now live a quiet lifestyle far from the fast track we'd been on.

I began writing again, and I started a freelance editing business. We found encouraging and teaching others what we had learned was fulfilling. I'd often wondered why God had brought us along this path—why he'd given us the skills and abilities we had if we were just to be retirees. What a waste, I thought. But he wasn't finished with us yet.

I now have a career coming alongside authors who are endeavoring to publish their work. I teach, train, and translate the ups and downs of the publishing world to them. My husband shares his business and Bible knowledge to build up other men. Because of our faith in God, we are happy and fulfilled, and look forward to our remaining years of service.

Skee Ball, Pizza Fights, and Fun!

I had been dating Roy for a while, and things were getting serious. He decided the time had come for me to meet his children, Jill and James. Very apprehensive but knowing this was the essential next step, I flew down from New Jersey to Atlanta with him.

You wouldn't think a six-year-old girl and a three-year-old boy could terrify a thirty-plus-year-old woman, would you? I'd never been around young kids much, other than an occasional babysitting job when I was in high school. And having the approval of these two meant everything.

We went to Chuckie Cheese for the afternoon and for dinner. Even though the place was warm, Jill wouldn't take off her plush, furry bear coat. Roy went off with James and left me with Jill. Oh, boy, what to do? She shook her head "no" at everything I suggested until skee ball.

We played skee ball for what seemed like an eternity, but when Roy and James came back, Jill had more winning tickets than anyone and had warmed up enough to the room (and to me) to take off her coat.

Their tradition at Chuckie Cheese was to have pizza (cut into kid-sized squares) and Cokes. After we'd devoured most of the pizza, Roy and Jill started a food fight with each other with the leftover pieces.

I was horrified—how could they behave like this in a public place! While scooting over to distance myself from the two of them, my sleeve caught on my Coke. The Coke tipped over, right into my lap. Now who was misbehaving! Laughing at myself and my clumsiness, and at the ridiculousness of the situation, I finally relaxed and enjoyed the rest of the evening.

Once we got back to the hotel, Roy suggested I stay for a while as he gave the kids their baths and got them ready for bed. The jacuzzi bathtub had one of those metal doors that turned the tub into a steam bath if you so desired. The kids thought shutting and opening the door was so much fun.

That night, unable to find the regular soap, Roy decided a shampoo bubble bath was in order. He and I went out to talk a bit while the kids had their bath. Suddenly, we heard Jill giggling and saying, "Daddy, Daddy! Come here!"

Roy went to see what was going on and cracked up. "Deb, you have to come see this!"

Going into the bathroom, I too got hysterical. The kids had overloaded the bath with shampoo, turned on the jacuzzi, and shut the door. Bubbles were climbing up the walls and the door and the kids had practically disappeared in the bubbles!

This family was one I could certainly fit into with my penchant for mishaps and love of funny situations. I'll never forget my introduction to the kids, skee ball, pizza fights, and fun.

LIGHT THAT FIRE!

On a romantic weekend in Carmel, my husband treated me to a suite overlooking the ocean at the Carmel Highlands Inn. The room was as exquisite as the view, with a fireplace, nice comfy chairs, and even a bottle of champagne from the manager.

We'd heard about the Inn from a friend we had visited in LA. Pete told us we definitely had to stay there on our drive up the coast. He went on to tell us when he and his wife were there, they sipped the champagne, lit the wood in the fireplace, admired the view, then lit another fire between themselves. As things were getting hotter, the smoke alarm went off … they were so embarrassed. We razzed them both, and we all laughed uproariously.

We had a beautiful drive up the coast. Touring the Hearst Castle was great and the Getty Museum was impressive. We finally arrived in Carmel and checked into the Inn.

Needless to say, history repeated itself … we admired the view, lit the fire in the fireplace, sipped the champagne, kindled the flames between us … and the smoke alarm went off.

After we stopped laughing and could talk, we called the front desk to say there was no fire—we'd forgotten to open the flue.

A very bored young man sighed. "Never mind, lady, happens all the time."

Our first trip together to California certainly had some high–"lights!"

Oh, I Get It!

"Hello," I said as I answered the phone.

"Deb, it's Diane," the voice on the line announced. "Is Roy there?

I handed my husband the phone, grabbed my coffee and sat down. The caller was my husband's ex-wife.

"Roy, they want to hold Jimmy back a year, " Diane told Roy. "His teacher says he's not ready for first grade. I don't understand. Jimmy loves school and wants to learn how to read."

Roy stood silently holding the phone. "Diane, you know that I'd love to help our son. I'm just not sure how I can, living so far away.

The conversation soon ended. With no solution in sight on how to help my stepson, Jimmy, Roy and I began to pray.

A few days later, while I was playing bridge with friends, I related Jimmy's woes.

"He sounds just like Kyle!" my friend Nancy exclaimed. "Maybe Jimmy learns differently too."

"What did you do about Kyle?" I asked, eager to find a solution.

"We took him to Dr. Gold. He's a great doctor, who is wonderful at getting at the heart of the problem with kids who learn differently."

That night, I shared Nancy's story with Roy. He was excited about the possibilities and called Diane. "Diane, why don't you send Jimmy here for a visit, so we can have him tested by Dr. Gold?"

A few days later, we were standing at the airport eagerly waiting to greet Jimmy. We had a wonderful night together, and the next day, we headed into New York City to meet Dr. Gold. Several hours passed before we heard the verdict. Jimmy did have learning problems. He both saw and heard things differently from most kids.

As Jimmy slept in the backseat on the way home, we agonized over a solution to the problem. Dr. Gold's recommendation was for Jimmy to work with a learning consultant and an occupational therapist. How was Diane, who worked full time, going to handle taking Jimmy to appointments several days a week?

After many long distance calls and much discussion, Diane made a very heroic, self-sacrificing choice. "Roy, you and Deb have the ability to care for Jimmy and the training nearby he needs. I don't. Why doesn't Jimmy live with you during the school year, and I can see him summers and school vacations?"

With that decision, a wonderful, blond-headed, eager little six-year old came to live with Roy and me. Many days of investigation later, we found the perfect specialists to work with Jimmy and a wonderful Montessori school.

Jimmy kept telling us, "I'm going to learn to read! I'm going to learn to read!" But at first, he didn't.

After months of little progress, we were all frustrated—Jimmy most of all. We prayed a breakthrough would occur, but as time limped by, the chances seemed slim. Then one spring day, a teacher from the school excitedly called us. "I think I found the solution! I was watching Jimmy work a maze. He studied it for a long time and then drew it perfectly. If I can show him the end results and how the letters fit together to get there, I think we can teach him to read."

Working with flower petals of consonants around a center of base words, she showed Jimmy how language worked. "See, Jimmy? This petal 'B' and the center of the flower 'at' spells *bat*. Add the petal 'C' and the center spells *cat*."

Jimmy's eyes lit up. "Oh, I get it! I get it! Then this is *mat*, and this is *rat*, and this is *sat*."

"Right, Jimmy."

"Then this is *man* and *can* and *ran* and *tan*." The breakthrough we'd prayed for had occurred. Jimmy was on his way.

Lots of time and patience, a perceptive doctor, a creative teacher, a self-sacrificing mom, a dad who wouldn't give up, a boy who wanted to learn, and me (a stepmom open to God's plans) all worked together to allow God to help this special child bloom.

RummiKub Summer

Jill and James flipped places during the summer. James, who lived with us during the school year, would go to visit his mom in Georgia. Jill, who lived with her mom during the school year, would come to spend the summers with us in New Jersey and later, Pennsylvania.

The separation of the kids was hard on all of us. James missed his mom, Jill missed James and the things he was able to do she couldn't. And we adults bore up the best we could.

Summers were tough for me. I'd finally learned to be around a little boy, but a little girl, especially a strong-willed little girl, was a challenge. I'm sure having her normal world turned upside down was tough on Jill too.

As both Roy and I were still working, Jill got to enjoy Country Day School and the summer activities there. When we all got home, we played games, watched movies, or just goofed off.

One summer, after I was working from home and Jill had grown too old for summer camp, we played games a lot. I'd grown up playing games with my parents and grandmother and would play for hours, whether I won or not.

RummiKub was my favorite game to play. The game was fast and, for me, fun. That summer, however, was a different story. We would play, and I would lose. The next day, the same story. By the end of the summer, Jill was ahead fifty-one games to one.

I still love the game—I don't think Jill has played RummiKub since!

Jimmy's Bike

"Oh, help! What am I going to do now?" My husband's six-year-old son, Jimmy, had just come to live with us. Have I mentioned I had no idea what to do with a little boy? I'd never been around kids at all, and I had a full-time job to keep me busy.

A few days after he arrived, he asked, "Can I play outside?"

Praying for wisdom, I said, "Okay, but be careful."

I found out later he'd gone up the hill, knocking on every door and asking, "Do you have any little boys for me to play with?" To his delight, he found a house at the top of the hill with not one, but two little boys. The boys had a great time playing together.

At the beginning of summer, both his friends received bicycles. My husband, Roy, promised Jimmy we would get him a bike too. However, Roy left town the next day on business.

The day after he left, Jimmy kept asking, "Are we going to get my bike now, Mom? Can we go now?

I stalled and stalled, hoping he would wait until his father got home, but at last I said, "Let's go look for a bike."

Off we went to Sears, where we looked at every single bike. Finally, he settled on a nice red one. But when they brought out our purchase, to my horror, it was unassembled! I prayed, "Oh, help, Lord! What am I going to do?"

Once we got the bike home, Jimmy said, "I want to ride my bike *now*, Mom!"

"Oh, Jimmy! I bought you the bike like you wanted. Can't you wait until tomorrow for Daddy to put it together?"

"No, Mom. I want to ride it now! You can put it together, I know you can!"

He had more faith in me than I did. What did I know about assembling a bicycle? We ripped into the carton. "Careful, Jimmy! We don't want to lose any of the pieces."

"Oh, boy! Oh, boy!" Jimmy danced around the family room. "My own bike!" My own bike! Hurry up, Mom!"

With great dread, I read the directions and set off to find the tools I needed to put it together. Fortunately (or perhaps unfortunately), the tools were right where they belonged. "I guess there's no putting this off!" I groused to myself.

Following the directions, I laid out the pieces and began to figure out how to connect them. Jimmy could hardly contain his excitement. Finally, after a couple of incorrect attempts and what seemed like hours, the completely assembled bike stood before us. I tightened a couple of bolts, not really sure it would hold up when Jimmy tried to ride it. Then we wheeled it outside through the garage where Jimmy mounted and rode the bike around the parking area.

"It works! It works! I knew you could do it! My very own bike!" Jimmy was in ecstasy. "I'm going to go show it to my friends," he said, pushing it up the hill.

When Roy got home the next evening, all he had to do was tighten a couple of bolts a bit more. How about that? I had put it together correctly. Imagine my surprise when a couple of days later, Jimmy's friends' mom related to me Jimmy was riding around the neighborhood bragging about his bike. "My bike's special. Mom built my bike!"

"Didn't you know that for an extra ten bucks, Sears would have assembled it for you?" she asked, laughing.

"They would have?" I could have saved myself all that agony, but how was I to know?

As I thought about the situation later, I mused perhaps this was what was supposed to have happened. I'd received a big lesson in the faith of a little child (and I'd learned I could do more than I knew I could). All things are possible with prayer and some encouragement!

EVEN ATLANTA

Life was good. I enjoyed my relationship with my husband and family. I enjoyed my work. I was walking closely with the Lord. There was just one little problem.

My husband was talking about moving back to Atlanta, where we'd each lived with previous spouses. He reasoned he'd see both of his children more frequently, and they'd be able to live together—part time with us and part time with their mother—instead of one with us and the other with her.

Atlanta held so many unhappy memories for me. Emotionally, I stomped my foot. "I do not want to go back to Atlanta!"

I sought a moment with God. "Thank you for all you have done for me, Lord—all the many blessings you have showered upon us. I want so much to walk in your will. I will do anything, go anywhere—whatever you want me to do."

Very quietly, yet very clearly, I heard him say to me, "Even Atlanta, Deb? Even Atlanta?"

I was speechless. I stopped praying.

Even Atlanta?

Did I really trust him that much? Did I really want to be totally in his will if it meant moving there?

Finally, I was able to respond. "If it's your will, Lord, that we move to Atlanta, I'm willing to go. I trust you with my life and with my family."

Later that night, as my husband and I talked, I told him I was willing to go back to Atlanta if he felt that was best for the family.

He never brought it up again.

What he and the Lord wanted was my willingness. I had to be willing to follow my husband as head of the family; I had to be willing to follow God's leading—even to the ends of the earth. Even to Atlanta.

Aloha, Hawaii

The summer before Jill turned sixteen, Roy and I decided to use all the frequent traveler points we had for airlines and hotels to take a cruise in Hawaii with the kids. Needless to say, everyone was excited about the trip and what we'd see and do.

We had points enough to make the long flight in First Class. The special attention the kids got from the flight attendants delighted us and helped make the flight seem shorter. By the time we got to Honolulu, we were wired and tired.

The next day, we boarded our ship for our cruise around the islands. We had a super special deal. Our travel agent had found out that the owner's suite was two hundred dollars a night less expensive than two staterooms. So we were going First Class the whole way.

Jill and James loved the free sodas and snacks we were given and ordering room service at any time during the day. We loved the spaciousness of the suite and our private bedroom.

But by far the most fun on our trip was the shore excursions. We took a helicopter ride over the Grand Canyon of Kauai. We toured a lava field on Oahu. The trip the kids never let me forget was our bus trip to a macadamia nut farm. As they were fond of relating, "We took a three-hour bus ride over a bumpy, dusty road to a place where we saw the trees and the factory where the macadamia nuts were being covered by Hershey's Chocolate! Really, Mom!"

One of the stops offered scuba diving trips. I love to scuba and got certified when I lived in Miami in my twenties. The two kids and I decided this would be great fun. We were trained on the equipment in a swimming pool at the hotel. James kept making fun of Jill, who was having a difficult navigating with the gear—James was doing great with his.

The dive boat took us out to the diving reef. Jill was the first one in the water and took to the sport like a fish. I was next in—scuba to me is one of the freest feelings in the world. Next was James. Practically a pro in the pool, he panicked in the ocean as soon as his head got underwater. After three tries, he gave up—not something our son often did. So he stayed with Roy on the boat while Jill and I had the time of our lives.

When we got home from Hawaii, Jill was still so enthralled with diving she took lessons in Pennsylvania, in rock quarries that were muddy and unclear. But she certified. I was so proud of her for taking a new found love and increasing her knowledge and proficiency in the sport.

P.S. Roy and James went windsurfing on a very windy day. To say they were underwater more than they were on top skimming along the waves is an understatement.

Relationships Are Everything

In 1985, I risked everything, left my well-paying corporate career, and launched Positive Connections© (formerly The Haggerty Group), my speaking and consulting business. My first two clients were first, a company I had worked with while at AT&T and second, one of the AT&T Sales Divisions. During my tenure at AT&T, I had carefully nurtured the relationships with these two groups. Nurturing means carefully tending, gently handling, and valuing the relationship. Valued relationships are to be cherished and cultivated so they grow strong and fruitful.

Luke 6:38 (NLT) teaches, "Give, and you will receive. Your gift will return to you in full—pressed down, shaken together to make room for more, running over, and poured into your lap. The amount you give will determine the amount you get back."

I became a student of relationships, something the business world calls networking. Networking is a process that can be learned and followed assiduously. There are four basic steps: Principle, Process, Place, and Practice. The Principle has been stated by the Scripture above. The next step is the Process.

Process: Determine the answers to the following questions:

- Why am I networking?
- With whom will I be networking?
- What am I able to give to the process?

- What do I hope to gain?
- When will I network?

Next, set goals for networking. Decide on a particular time of day or the week when you will proactively network. Set up a system for tracking the contacts you make, whether paper or computer-based. Prepare the tools of networking: business cards, thank you notes, brochures. Make sure your materials are professional and reflect you. Remember, you want to make positive connections!

Place: Where can you network? The possibilities are endless!

- Chambers of Commerce
- Writers' Conferences
- Social Clubs and Churches
- Networking Groups
- Professional Associations
- PTA
- Charitable Organizations

In other words, networking can happen any time in any place with anyone.

I once was standing in the lobby of a hotel in Charleston waiting for the airport shuttle to arrive. Gazing around the lobby, I spied a woman taking a beautiful silver and royal blue necklace from a shopping bag and looking at it admiringly. Those are my favorite colors, so I exclaimed to her, "My, what a pretty necklace!"

We began one of those hotel lobby or airport waiting area conversations we sometimes have with people whom we will never see again. She asked me if I was going to the airport, and if so, would I like to share the car she had coming? I gratefully accepted her invitation.

As we were loading our luggage into the car, she chirped to me, "And what do you do?"

My spirits plummeted. I was tired from a long trip, I didn't want to go into sales mode, so I tried to be brief. "I'm a professional speaker, but I wasn't here speaking. I was helping a friend."

"Oh, really!" she exclaimed. "I come to these conferences looking for speakers for my company!"

My inner voice sighed. *Why now, Lord? I'm so tired. I don't want to do this.*

We got into the car, and as we glided off to the airport, she asked, "What do you speak about?"

I handed her my business card and mumbled my speeches were listed on the back.

She read down the list of talks and asked, "Right Person, Right Job—what's that all about?"

At that point, I gave up and realized I was getting into the conversation whether I wanted to or not. I explained that many of my consulting clients had been burned in the hiring/firing process, that I had found some objective assessments to use in the process, and that the speech taught a better methodology for hiring employees.

"Really!" she excitedly interrupted. "I have to hire someone next week, and I can't afford to make a mistake! Please overnight me the marketing materials for these assessments."

When I got home, I sent her the materials. She liked them and purchased the software and the assessments. Next, she hired me to come out and spend two days with her department to facilitate teambuilding in the group. The day I returned from that engagement, I got a call from another group in the same company asking when I could come back and do the same for them!

Five little words brought me almost two-thirds of my revenue for the year—and brought me a new friendship.

Business Suits to Bunny Slippers

As I left my excellent corporate job to start my own consulting company in 1985, I left with stars in my eyes and dreams that were soaring. I knew I would quickly become a successful consultant with many clients all clamoring for my services. More than that, I'd be able to work at home and lose the long commute. I'd be able to have casual Friday every day unless I was seeing clients.

Alas, I very quickly discovered clients were not beating down my door, real stars only come out at night, and dreams could quickly crash. What I discovered was the "solo" life was not all it was cracked up to be. There were several challenges I had not considered but would have to overcome to become successful. These are not easy steps, but if you follow in my path, you will have a start on having it MADE.

Motivation

When I left to start my own company, my major motivation was escaping from the environment I was in. I had been in a company-creation role in my previous position and assumed I would be equally successful in creating my own company. I also imagined the money I would be earning—two to three times my salary, I was sure.

I had done no real research, had not checked out the competition, and had not assessed my own reasons for going solo. I quickly discovered that escape from one endeavor is not a good motivator for the next—you should be moving toward something you greatly desire. Money is not a great motivator either—most of us predict greater earnings in the early years than we ever see, I bought office furniture, a computer, letterhead, and other stationery items needed, had a logo designed, and then looked around and remarked, "Oops, no clients." I need to look inside myself to discover what my real motivation was for continuing this newly created business.

ATTITUDE

I had a great attitude when I left my old company. The sky was the limit. I was positive I could do anything. But in a very real world, there are "dream-busters"—those people in our immediate circle who say, "How could you possibly have left such a great job?" "What can you possibly offer as a consultant that is not already available?" "How are you going to get clients?" "What are your rates going to be?" "How can you live on that?"

I had answers to none of the questions, and my attitude quickly shifted from positive to negative. "What have I done?" "What could I possibly have been thinking?" These questions stonewalled me, and I lost momentum, all my efforts grinding to a halt. I needed to keep my dreams and goals in front of me, to realize there would be ups and downs in the journey, but to remind myself the trip was still worth traveling. I needed to realize rejections were not of me personally but were for my sales or consulting roles. I needed to practice telling people who I was and what I was about if I hoped to sell them on utilizing my services. I needed to stay positive.

DISCIPLINE

Ouch! I hate that word! One of the first things I discovered was playing solitaire on my computer was much easier than making sales calls. Wandering out to the kitchen and picking up a snack was much easier than working on a direct mail piece. To pick up the phone and call folks back at my old office was easier than to get out of my office to call on prospects.

Easier though those activities may have been, they did not (and do not) bring in clients! I had to set daily, even hourly, objectives for myself, then reward myself if I accomplished them. I had to get out of bed and go to my office even if I was tired and wanted to sleep longer. I had to keep educating myself to keep current in my field. I had to learn to be my own secretary and mail person and boss.

You need a great deal of stick-to-it-iveness to be successful as an entrepreneur. Another discovery was this was not an eight-to-five job; this was ten, twelve hours a day, five and six days a week. Self-discipline was mandatory if I was to even begin, much less succeed, in my endeavor.

ENCOURAGEMENT

When I worked for the large company, there were always people around. Someone was always dropping in to chat or to discuss an idea or to brainstorm with me. I loved the camaraderie of the group: the give and take, the bantering back and forth that continually went on. To my horror, I discovered when I went solo, solo means alone! I don't do well without people around. I was lonely. I even became quite conversant with our dog!

To meet the need for people, as well as to make contacts who could become clients, I needed to get out of my office—to go where people were. I joined a couple of networking groups: one specifically for women business owners, another where leads were the order of the day. I joined the Chamber of Commerce and participated in its training and its networking events. Now I had the camaraderie I had been lacking in my home office, AND I had solitude to work when I needed it.

I learned some hard lessons when I traded in my business suits for bunny slippers. I learned if you are to go solo, you must have MADE several decisions: What is your motivation? How is your attitude? Will you be able to handle the dream-busters and the rejections that will undoubtedly occur? Are you disciplined enough to work on your own, without having to report your progress to someone else? Where will you get the encouragement and the energy to go on? If you can answer these questions, have a viable business idea and sufficient financing, you may be well on your way to having it MADE.

Looking back, I realize I was in no way prepared to go solo. Times were tough for many years. But now, I wouldn't trade where I am for anything. God always has a plan, even when we can't see the outcome at the time.

> Come now, you who say, "Today or tomorrow we will go into such and such a town and spend a year there and trade and make a profit"— yet you do not know what tomorrow will bring. (James 4:13-14a)

No Longer the Ugly Stepmother

Mother love is the fuel that enables a normal human being to do the impossible.—Marion C. Garretty

When Jimmy came to live with us when he was six, I was delighted to help raise this cute, blond-headed little boy. Over the years, little Jimmy became James. By the time he was sixteen, he was a surly, obnoxious, foul-mouthed teenager. Oh, how I wished for that cuddly boy in pajamas to return. Why did I ever think I could cope with a boy? When did he transmute into "The Enemy" and I into "The Ugly Stepmother?"

Roy was often out of the country on business. I was coping the best I could with James, but I was really struggling. I functioned as Mom's Taxi Service. Once he called me to pick him up with his best friend, Colin, at their favorite skateboarding place. But when I got to that location—no James, no Colin. Finally my cell phone rang.

"Where are you, Mom?"

"I'm right where you said you'd be—where are you?"

"Oh, Colin and I decided to get a hamburger—we're down the hill at Burger King."

This scene was followed by James yelling and swearing at me when I confronted him with my frustration. The argument that followed I imagine takes place in many a stepparent's household.

"As long as you are in our house, you will obey our rules!"

"This is my dad's house, and I don't have to listen to you!"

"I am your father's wife, and I am in charge while he is gone!"

"I'm leaving this f–ing place!"

James uttered those words to me and stormed downstairs to his room. In a panic, I locked the door to downstairs and frantically called his father. What would I do if James ran away while Roy was gone?

Thank goodness, I reached Roy. As calmly as I could, I explained what had happened. He asked to speak with James. I called James to the phone and left the room. Later, Roy called me back and said all was okay, and he'd be home the next day. I found out when he arrived that he'd placated James and sided with him on the argument.

From that point on, I had no control over James or any say in what he was or wasn't allowed to do. I felt like an unwelcome stranger in my own home.

The year James was a senior in high school, he was assigned to the "worst" English teacher. All of the kids had to do a research paper, which would extend over most of the school year. Roy pleaded with me to help James with the project. "You're so good at writing—you'll know just how to help him put it together. You know how he struggles with things like this."

Flattered at being asked to help for a change, I agreed. The first part of the project was to pick a book. James picked *Deliverance*. Then he picked a thesis and scoured the library and the internet for research. The night before his research cards were due, he was up until three a.m. finishing them. He then drove them to a friend's house for her to deliver in class as we were going away on a trip, and he had an excused absence. When he returned to class after the trip, the teacher ridiculed him about having someone else turn in his cards: "You just wanted to play hooky!"

The outline and thesis statement were next. James and I worked for hours to get them just right. Finally, I went to bed while he finished. The next morning, I found on my desk one of the rewards a stepmother often dreams of but seldom receives. A letter from James read ...

> Mom,
>
> Thanks so much for helping me on this project. I just know that we'll get a really high grade on it. There isn't any way to tell you how much I appreciate it.
>
> Love, your son, James

I cried as I showed Roy the letter.

We anxiously awaited his grade on the outline—it came back 0! And next to his thesis statement was the scrawl, "Who cares?" James was demoralized, and I was furious!

"What kind of a teacher is this? Does he call this a critique? How is James supposed to know what is wrong? And besides, there isn't anything wrong with this!"

My husband was equally incensed. He wanted to head into school to confront the teacher. James told us about all the negative and slanderous comments the teacher had been making about him in front of the class, as well as several inappropriate stories the teacher had told the students.

"In fact," James told us, "several times he's said in front of the class that no matter what I do, I'm not going to pass!"

Now deadly calm, I told my husband that confronting this particular teacher would not help—I would go and talk to the principal.

A day later, I was in the principal's office armed with my arguments on James's behalf. The principal made the major mistake of trying to patronize me. I assured him I knew what I was talking about—that I'd been an English major in college and had my MBA—in addition to being a published author. He backpedaled frantically. I told him we wanted James transferred to another section of English with a different teacher.

He assured me that was not possible and that James had probably just overreacted. This teacher, he related, was one of the best, though on the tough side.

I asked him if he thought constructive criticism was part of a teacher's job on a project such as this.

"Oh, it's one of the most important parts!"

"Then explain to me how this fits with constructive criticism?"

I showed him the outline with the teacher's comment.

"And let me show you how James felt about it before he got this back." I showed him my prized letter.

Crestfallen, the principal admitted there was nothing constructive in what James had been given. I repeated our desire to have James transferred. He reiterated a change was not possible. I told him all James needed to graduate was a passing grade in English. I was not going to allow him to prevent my son from graduating even if I had to pull James out of school and homeschool him! I further informed the principal I was sure the PTA would love to hear about this teacher and that I had other parents who were willing to testify about the treatment their kids had received when in this teacher's class.

Finally he capitulated and agreed to move James to another class.

While relating my conversation to Roy and James later, I could see the incredulity on James's face. His stepmom had done the impossible! No one went up against this teacher and won—no one had ever been transferred out, despite frequent attempts.

At that point a transformation occurred in our relationship. I started to see James as a person trying very hard to succeed given the obstacles he had to overcome. He started to see me as a person who loved him and really wanted to help and to be a part of his life.

While our relationship did not become smooth overnight, things did become better. He became a bright young man earnestly working to be a success at his job.

Another "reward" I received occurred when James was building his first house.

He called me and asked, "Mom, will you come and meet with the designer with me to pick out the options? You're so good at that." We spent a delightful morning doing the planning for his house and then had a very gracious lunch.

I saw my son as a very special person and not "The Enemy." He saw me as a friend and not "The Ugly Stepmother." In fact, the birthday card I got from him that year said, "For My Mother. One kindness follows another, and you are the source. You give advice when it's asked for, encouragement when it's needed, and kindness when it means the most. I hope you'll always know how much that means to me."

Yes, James, I knew. I hope you knew how much you meant to me. I am proud to have been considered your mother. You were one of the greatest challenges of my life, and you were one of its greatest rewards.

THE SPIRIT OF SANTA CLAUS

Early in 1998, my beloved dad had to be placed in a nursing home. Alzheimer's Disease was stealing away his memories and his ability to function on his own. I was heartbroken—I knew this meant the end of the daddy that I'd known. I couldn't conceive of him not being there for me as he'd always been. He was so cheerful, happy, and always had a "Howdy!" and a kind word for everyone he met.

At Christmas time in my hometown, and then when my parents first moved to Florida, Daddy played Santa Claus during the holidays at various shopping centers for many years. He loved to watch the eyes of the kids as they met Santa and told him what they wanted for Christmas. At the time, I lived in Orlando where Walt Disney World is located. I found a Santa hat with Mickey Mouse ears I brought to Dad when we visited him on what was to be his last Christmas.

He was thrilled! Even though Alzheimer's was messing with his mind, he immediately remembered he was Santa! He insisted Mom find and help him on with his red flannel shirt.

He put on the hat and said, "I've got to go entertain the girls!" He then shuffled out to the nurses' station on his wing. He grinned at them and proceeded to do a little jig—he captivated the whole group! In fact, they were so enthralled, they even took pictures. A couple of them even sat on his lap!

In late February, when we became aware Dad was to be with us just a little bit longer, word quickly spread around the nursing home. During the three days before he passed away, every nurse and aide in the home who had ever cared for him came to his room to say goodbye. One by one, they stopped in for a minute, patted his hand, paused, and then left.

We held a memorial service for Daddy about a week after his death. We knew there would be a huge outpouring of friends and business associates at the service. Daddy never knew a stranger and touched so many lives during his lifetime. He was always ready with a cheerful word if that was what was needed. But what said even more about the kind of man he was and the people who loved him was the attendance of Daddy's favorite nurse and aide at the service. Daddy even opened the hearts of those people who take care of patients like him every day—staff unlikely to attend the funeral of an eighty-nine-year-old patient who has died.

Daddy left sunshine everywhere he went, even the nursing home where he resided for his last year of life. The spirit of giving and helping others never left my dad while he was alive. I doubt anything is different now that his home is in Heaven. He's probably still making friends with everyone he meets and playing Santa Claus.

To Dad

My dad is leaving me
I never thought he would.
He was always there for me
Every time he could.

He was such a special guy
Had stories without end.
I never thought that he would die
I never thought his world would end.

My daddy was so special
He still is to me.
But now he's dying, he's leaving
My mom, his grandkids, and me.

I don't want him to go
I'm going to miss him so.
But, Lord, I know that there with you
He'll be at peace and healthy too.

Father, keep my daddy close
'Though I am quite morose.
I know that you'll take care of him … and me
You died for both of us upon that tree.

You're so awesome, Father
You never make mistakes.
Lord, I love you deeply
With every breath I take.

I know that this was best for Dad
I let him go—although I'm sad.
Mom and I will grieve some more
Until we meet again—at heaven's door.

Instant Friends, Sisters for Life

How do you know? One minute you're meeting a stranger and the next, you know you've met your "new best friend!" Kathy is such a friend. We met in 1998 in a neighborhood Bible study. I didn't really know anyone in the group and erroneously assumed everyone else knew each other.

When we finished the "coffee and chat," we gathered in the family room. Several of us sat on a sectional sofa, one on a chair at the end, while Kathy sat in a rocker across from the coffee table. Somehow, that didn't feel right—she seemed to be separated from us. Patting the sofa beside me, I beckoned to Kathy. "Come, sit beside me. There's room." Smiling, she rose and joined us.

That simple gesture began a friendship more akin to having a sister. We've shared food and stories and frustrations and tears and encouragement. When one of us is shopping, we frequently check to see if the other needs something to save her the trip—and money has never changed hands. Though we sometimes disagree, we both know this blessing of friendship God gifted us with will survive through the years.

We see each other infrequently now—we live in different states. We're not as up on what's happening in each others' lives. But when we are together, we are instantly in tune with each other just as we were so many years ago. Kathy will always be one of my bestest friends.

Coincidences? Not a Chance!

What a great evening Kathy and I had—lots of laughing and "remember whens." After she left, I turned out the lights and headed to bed. When the telephone rang, I assumed Kathy had forgotten something and answered.

"Deb?" I heard the voice of my son's roommate on the other end.

"Yes, it's me."

"Deb—there's been an accident! James is dead."

"NO, NO! Are you sure? Are you there?" I shouted at him in my shock.

"Yes, there's no mistake—I saw the car. My cousin and his wife were in it. They are fine—not a scratch."

"What happened—are you sure?"

"Yes, I'm sure—he missed a curve and flipped the car. He didn't have his seatbelt on and the Targa top was open—he was killed instantly."

"I've got to go—I have to call Roy." Hanging up, I sank to the floor—what would we do?

The call all parents dread and pray never occurs. My husband had been anticipating it for years—ever since James got his driver's license. Now Roy was overseas in Belgium—and I'd received the awful news! My heart breaking, I placed the call.

"Honey ... I don't know how to tell you ... there's been an accident ... James didn't make it. He's ... he's dead."

"NOOOOOOOOOOOOOO!"

I never want to hear that sound in my husband's voice again. He brokenly said he'd get the first flight home.

Praying, sobbing, I called Kathy—knowing she'd be asleep, because she always took a sleeping pill. She answered the phone! God was with me and already working his wonders.

"Kathy, I need you—James has been killed in an accident!"

"I'll be right there—don't worry—I'll be there!"

Still sobbing, but mind working overtime, I knew I had to call James's mother. Rocky, his stepdad, was shocked.

"I'll tell Diane. Does Jill know?"

"I'll call her now. When I know more, I'll call you back."

Oh, how I dreaded making the call to Jill—she and James were so close and had even shared an apartment. I reached her husband—I could hear Jill sobbing in the background—obviously Roy or James's roommate had already reached her. I told Brian that I'd call as soon as I knew more.

"Deb?" Kathy knocked on the door. "Deb? Let me in." I unlocked the door and collapsed into her arms.

"Oh, Kathy! What will we do? What will Roy do? James was not only his son, but also his best friend!"

"Don't worry about that—have you heard from the police?"

"No. I guess I could call and see if it's true—but it has to be. Jill already knew!"

As I picked up the phone, the doorbell rang. There stood a uniformed policeman. My heart sank—it *was* true. He came in, told us the circumstances, gave his condolences, and left a number for us to get more information.

Roy called back. "I got a flight on Ryan Air—they're leaving for home in just a few hours. I'll be on the flight. My car is at the airport. I'll be there as soon as I can."

Kathy and I just hugged each other. She went to make us a cup of coffee. We had lots to do. Unfortunately, Roy's mom and both our dads had died within the last few years, so I was all too familiar with the details that needed handling.

I couldn't sleep. I posted the sad news on Facebook asking for prayers for all of us—that God would facilitate all we needed to do. I prayed for strength—I knew the burden of the arrangements would fall on me.

Immediately, responses started pouring ... "praying!" "Oh, Deb!" "My heart is breaking for you!" "God will get you through this." My friend Georgia later told me when she read the post, she'd immediately started praying Roy and I, and our marriage, would survive James's death.

The next morning, Kathy fielded all my calls as I started making arrangements. She kept everyone out until Roy got home. She called the police station to get the police report and handled the insurance calls. I called our pastor to let him know.

When Roy arrived several hours later, he just hugged me and sobbed. I'd never seen him cry before—even when his mom died. I told him the basics of the accident. He related that he'd been jet-lagged and had arisen an hour early—he'd *just* turned on his phone when I called. The *only* flight that flew nonstop to Orlando that *week* was the one on which he'd flown home.

Taking care of the details, I let him mourn. He talked with his daughter—his ex-wife and her husband. Kathy was constantly there. We made arrangements for the funeral home to pick

James up after the autopsy. He'd be cremated and buried next to his grandparents. We took care of the insurance and letting his office know. A memorial service was arranged in the town where James lived so his friends could say goodbye. I wrote the order of service and arranged for our pastor and his family to come give the eulogy and sing.

We drove to Jacksonville and rode in a caravan past the place he'd been killed, stopping to place a wreath and a picture—his friends had wanted to do that for him. We played the Elvis Presley version of "Battle Hymn of the Republic." His roommate had told us the song was James's favorite.

At the memorial service, many of his friends gave their remembrances. We were touched many of our friends had come up by van from Orlando to be with us. Instead of flowers, we'd requested Gideon Bibles be given in James's memory. Over seven hundred fifty were donated! What an impact his death would potentially have on others.

On a gloomy day in June, we buried our only son in the cemetery in Plymouth—a dozen roses decorating his grave. James always bought roses for his girlfriends—but he'd get me to pay for them. This was so bittersweet. They'd be the last roses I'd buy for him.

So much happened providentially I knew God had been there in the details—from Kathy being awake, to Roy turning on his phone, to his flight home being available that day, to my being able to do the necessary tasks, to everyone attending all of the events, to our having seen James the weekend before, to Roy and I drawing closer together instead of being pulled apart.

I'll never stop missing James—but I do know he's with his Lord in heaven. Happy memories of our times together will keep me smiling. We'll see him again, and he'll greet us with that special grin of his when we arrive. God is always good.

I don't believe in coincidences, but God-cidences do happen every day.

Distress Signal

In my distress I called to the Lord, and he answered me. (Isaiah 2:1 NIV)

"In *my* distress I called to the Lord ..."

The year 1999 had been tough. My father and my father-in-law died, my business was not doing well, my husband traveled most of the time, and I was alone. Alone with my thoughts, worries, and fears, I struggled to endure from day to day.

In my *distress* I called to the Lord ...

December 13, 1999. The technician at the mammography center was chirpy. "Ninety-five percent of the time, the screening shows nothing."

Calmly, I replied, "But my doctor ordered an ultrasound and a diagnostic mammogram."

"Oh, we don't do those unless there's a problem."

"But my doctor ordered them!"

"I told you we don't do them unless there's a problem."

Irritated, I snarled, "Okay, they hurt! Is that enough of a problem?"

She smashed my breasts in the mammography machine. For the first time ever, the process hurt. She took the films to develop them.

In a short time, she was back, stern and serious. "We need to do more films."

I knew at that moment I had breast cancer.

"In my distress, I called to the Lord, and he ***answered*** me."

My doctor called before I got home from the center, wanting to see me.

The next day, she showed me the films. Where the tumor was located was low down on the left and near the chest wall. If the mammo technician had not slammed me, the cancer might not have been found until it was too late.

Finally, the doctor asked, "How attached are you to your breasts?"

Looking down, then looking at her, I said, "Well, they're not fastened on with Velcro!"

She collapsed in laughter. "I'm supposed to be comforting you!"

"In my distress I called to the Lord, and he answered ***me***."

The year 2000 was my journey down the path so many women have trod, the path of breast cancer. Yet, this time was one of the greatest blessings in my life. I received dozens of encouraging notes letting me know how much I was loved and prayed for. Through email, I was able to share my journey and minister to others. I learned there is strength in weakness, comfort in being comforted. And I was victorious and will live victoriously until proven otherwise. God is so good!

And the Comfort Overflows

Praise be to the God and Father of our Lord Jesus Christ, the Father of compassion and the God of all comfort, who comforts us in all our troubles, so that we can comfort those in any trouble with the comfort we ourselves receive from God. For just as we share abundantly in the sufferings of Christ, so also our comfort abounds through Christ (2 Cor 1:3-5 NIV).

"… who comforts us in all our troubles."

What a blessing this was for me. I really needed comfort. After seasons of trying, we'd accepted that getting pregnant was apparently impossible for us. I reveled in that verse and let the "God of all comfort" comfort me. I took an assignment in the nursery at church where I could get the "baby fix" I needed and be of service too. Finally, my heart was eased, and I was at peace.

Then God taught me the rest of the verse: "So that we can comfort those in any trouble with the comfort we ourselves have received from God." A woman in the church was also having difficulty conceiving, and she was literally driving herself crazy. Somehow, she and I became friends, and I was able to comfort her. And praise to him, after she became contented with her situation, she became pregnant and now has two boys to grace her life.

I'd often thought of this verse—and the situations that flowed from it—when it became oh so relevant again. I was diagnosed with breast cancer. My friends comforted me and put my name on their prayer chains. The number of people who emailed to say they were praying or who just offered words of encouragement blessed me. I started writing "Updates from Deb" to keep everyone up to date on what was going on. And the comfort became comfort for others. The email updates were forwarded to others who had friends or relatives with breast cancer.

One of the emails I received said, "My mother has breast cancer. She is three weeks behind you and was terrified. Since reading your updates, she is no longer afraid as you explained what happens so clearly." Many other similar notes followed— and the comfort truly overflowed.

Father, thank you for being Abba Father, the Daddy whose arms we can run into when we need comfort.

CHECKERBOARD HAIR

The evening of the day my hair started to fall out, Christie, Barbara, and I were having dinner at one of our favorite restaurants. Naturally, I had to tell them how it all happened.

"Guess what happened this morning?"

"What happened, Deb?" Christie asked, leaning forward in anticipation.

"I reached up to pull some fuzz out of my hair, and the whole clump of hair came out. I'm losing my hair!"

"Wow! What did you do?"

"I kept pulling pieces from different places on my head— then I showered and washed my hair to see how much more would come out."

Christie was fascinated. Barbara was unnaturally quiet.

"You know what would be fun?" I said, "Let's go back to my house after dinner, sit on the deck, and see if we can make a checkerboard pattern on my head!"

"How can you talk like that!!?" Barbara shouted at us. Our heads whipped around as we looked at her with astonishment. "She's losing her hair! That's terrible!" Barbara was near tears.

"It's just her hair, Barbara," Christie murmured soothingly. But Barbara was not to be comforted. She had too many friends who had cancer—the reminder that I was another was the last straw.

I didn't realize right away that many women would be distraught about losing their hair. I had to learn about it from others. Hair loss seemed to be the final straw. We lose our breast(s), our energy, our stamina—why our hair too?

When I spoke at a conference not long ago about my experiences, one of the women from the audience told me how it was for her. She just shook her head, "I couldn't bear to lose my hair. It's who I am. My whole image of me is wrapped up in how I look with my hair!" Her hair was her identity—losing it meant losing herself to the disease.

I was lucky that way. My image isn't tied to the way my hair looks. In fact, one of my favorite pictures of me from that time shows me bald with a full set of braces and glasses instead of contacts (chemo interfered with my contacts). For me, one of the hardest adjustments was not being able to do all the things I was used to doing.

I hated the "nap attacks" and not being able to just get up and go do the things I love to do. I found that my identity was tied up in being a doer. Not doing was hard, and having to ask for help was harder, much harder for me than worrying about how my hair looked.

Even so, losing my hair meant something else many of us with cancer have to deal with. Until we lose our hair, most of us look fairly normal. Losing our hair is the step that firmly sets us apart from the rest of the population. Of course, I always had fun with it. I walked into a hair salon with a friend one day and told the shocked patrons [my friend Eva Marie's story about that incident is also here in the book] that I was there for a permanent!

We'll always be separated from non-cancer folks. Once you've had breast cancer, even if you're free of symptoms for years, you know that the disease can always recur. As a friend said to me, "Once you've had breast cancer, you can't be sure it won't come back until you die of something else."

That's the shadow that's always lurking around the corner. It's also the reality that puts other things, like being bothered by asking for help—or losing your hair—into perspective.

For me, the hair issue was easily solved. A few days after that dinner with Christie and Barbara, I decided to shave my head.

First, I went to the beauty parlor and got "buzzed." Then I went home and borrowed my husband's shaving cream and razor and shaved the stubble off to be truly bald. When the hair started to grow back in, as I was still on chemo, I shaved again—amazing how many different directions hair grows!

I didn't stay bald, but I did find I liked short hair. Everyone who gets breast cancer has lots of hard things they have to deal with. But for me, checkerboard hair was one of the easy ones.

A Special Kind of Encouragement

When I was on my breast cancer journey, I never really considered how my family was handling my having the disease. You tend to become very self-centered when you could be fighting for your life.

Initially, Roy told me I could go ahead and have a mastectomy. I told him I had already decided that as well as I would have chemo but not radiation. I went to most of my chemo treatments alone or with a friend. Not until I was almost through with them did I ask him to come with me. When I ended up with a hysterectomy two months later, a friend came and stayed with me my first night after surgery—paying forward what someone had done for her. Roy was almost totally blocked out. Now I know how unkind that was—I was turning away my biggest supporter and friend.

Jill was very affected by my bout of cancer too. Perhaps we women identify with the progress and problems of the disease more than men do. I remember several encouraging telephone calls and a refrigerator magnet she sent me. I seldom recall being as touched as I was by this gift, which read:

Women Who Change the World

There are women who make things better ... simply by showing up. There are women of wit and wisdom who—through strength and courage—make it through. There are women who change the world every day ... women like you. —Ashley Rice

I still have the magnet—twenty years later.

Through Good Times and Bad

When I was diagnosed with breast cancer, I emailed a very few close friends to let them know. One friend who was not on the list emailed me to say, "We're your friends in the bad times as well as the good!"

As a result, I wrote to two lists of friends, whom I dubbed SuperGirls and PowerPals. I gave them permission to pass on my email to anyone they felt it would help.

The list grew over the next six months from those fourteen to over two hundred because people kept forwarding the email to others, who in turn forwarded to still others. I sent "Updates from Deb" periodically to describe what I was going through, so they could understand the tests and procedures.

Six months later, I'd received over thirteen hundred email messages back. Two of my favorites were "Because of your updates and courage, my mom went to have a mammogram for the first time in four years!" and "I was diagnosed six weeks behind you—I am following your emails closely so I know what to expect. Please continue to write your updates."

I've realized breast cancer was a blessing and not a curse. Discovering people truly care about me was wonderful, but being able to help others going through something similar was awesome!

MUSIC OF THE TUBE

Early in February 2000, while everybody else was getting ready for Valentine's Day, I was getting ready for a full battery of tests, including my first MRI. I was in a bit of a funk.

Previously that week, I'd received the reports from a pelvic ultrasound my doctor had recommended. The *lesions* he'd seen on the CT scan I'd had recently seemed to be cysts, but he wasn't sure. One ovary was greatly enlarged by this *mass*.

I had done a lot of research on the internet and had talked with my doctor. I knew this might be more cancer. Breast cancer and ovarian cancer often go hand in hand.

I was devastated. I had been feeling really good about making a great recovery from breast cancer surgery, but now a hysterectomy seemed to be in my future.

Moping around the house on Tuesday night, all of Wednesday, and Wednesday night, I thought about maybe having a whole new kind of cancer. I didn't even get dressed. Finally, I found the strength to call the doctor to schedule more tests.

Thursday, I was in a much better mood. I'd taken some action and scheduled the tests for Friday. Plus, I was thinking about all my friends who were there for me and praying for me. Life might not be good, but with friends and faith it usually doesn't stay too bad for too long.

By now, I was used to tests, so I wasn't nervous about most of them. They started Friday morning at 7:30, long before I usually even get up. The first test was the MRI. The prospect made me nervous.

I'm just a little bit claustrophobic, and the idea of being stuck inside a really small space was scary. But the staff did everything they could to make me comfortable.

They covered me with a blanket for warmth and gave me ear plugs for the noise they said I would hear. Then they gently pushed me into a narrow tube. The quick look I took showed about five to six inches of space between my face and the tube.

I kept my eyes shut most of the time! One time, though, I opened my eyes and found light glowed inside the tube, at least above my face. That helped. Don't ask me why, but I didn't really feel closed in.

Then the MRI started: Tap, tap, tap—like a drummer counting cadence on the rim of a snare drum. Then loud discordant sounds—sort of a doo-wop, doo-wop, doo-wop coupled with a low pitched busy signal.

This went on for what seemed like about ten minutes. Slight pause, tap, tap, tap, and different pitches of static like you get on a TV station after it goes off the air. I kept myself amused trying to imagine what tones would be next.

Then I was wheeled out, given a dye injection, and wheeled back in for "three more sets!" By then I was used to the sounds, and listened to the "music"—I even got to see some of the pictures. They looked pretty to me, but I would have to wait until the following week for results.

So I set off for the rest of the day's tests, with one more thing I could check off life's list. I had had my first MRI and survived by listening to the strange "music of the tube."

Six Feet Tall—And Bald

Friends are the spice of life and one of my best friends forever is Eva Marie Everson, noted speaker, Bible teacher, and author of many award-winning books. While I was walking my path of breast cancer, Eva Marie wrote this story about one of our adventures.

"Would you like to meet for lunch?" my friend Deb asked. "I'm going to be in your part of the world on Thursday, and I thought it'd be nice to get together."

Although Deb and I live in the same city, there's a forty-five minute distance between us. It seems we're always looking for excuses to "get together."

"I'd love to," I answered.

My valiant friend was successfully battling cancer. Chemo's only visible side effect had been the loss of a full head of hair. "I don't mind," I assured her.

A few days later, I sat across the table from Deb in a booth at a local restaurant where we exchanged news about our families, our work, and ourselves. She sat straight and tall as overhead lights cast reflections and halos about her head, completely unfettered from the questioning stares from other patrons. "I'm determined to get through this with grace and humor," Deb told me. "So far … so good."

"Excuse me," our waitress said from the side of our table, looking at Deb, "Do you mind if I ask if you have cancer? Are you undergoing chemo?"

"Yes, I am," Deb answered.

"Would you mind going to the hair salon a few shops down the mall?"

Our brows shot straight up. *Do what?*

"My friend, the owner, was just diagnosed with cancer … and she's not handling it well."

Deb smiled. "I'd be happy to!"

"I know you don't even know her," the waitress continued.

"I always say there are no strangers in the world, just new friends I've yet to meet," Deb countered. "Don't worry. Leave everything to me."

An hour later, I followed along as Deb, nearly six feet tall and completely bald, walked into the salon. "I'm here for a perm," she exclaimed to the gawking faces. Then she laughed. "I'd like to speak to the owner, please."

A petite, dark-haired woman approached. "I'm the owner," she said. "May I help you?"

Deb asked if there was a place they could talk. "Someplace private?"

I could sense the woman was nervous. Why would a bald woman want to talk to the owner of a small hair salon? To buy a wig, perhaps? Hopefully not to complain about a hair product gone bad.

"Sure," she said, then escorted us to the back where— among stacks of papers and boxes of shampoos and conditioners—a small desk was flanked by a few chairs. "Will this do?" she asked.

Deb and I sat, and Deb got right to the point. "Your friend from Gleason's Restaurant asked me to come down and speak with you. I have cancer."

The shop owner, whose name tag read "Maria,"* sat down. "I was just diagnosed," she said.

(*name changed)

"I know," Deb replied, her voice steady. "I want to talk with you about that."

For the next half hour, Deb shared her story, and then answered Maria's questions. Shoulders, straight with tension when we'd first sat down, were now relaxing. In no time, Maria was laughing at Deb's anecdotes and sharing some of her own more humorous moments of dealing with the disease they shared. Finally Deb asked, "Can we pray with you?"

Maria nodded. "Please."

We prayed together and were then escorted from the back of the shop, past the boxes of stored product, and down a wide aisle between sinks and salon chairs. All eyes were on us, questioning: *What was so funny back there?*

Just as we were about to reach the front door, it swung open and a distinguished gentleman walked in. After one look at Deb, he stopped short.

"I'd run the other way if I were you," Deb said, loud enough for everyone to hear. "When I came in, I had long hair. All I asked for was a trim!" She ran her hand over her smooth, shining head.

"What?" the man squawked.

"Seriously," Deb answered, never blinking nor missing a beat.

"Hey," Maria called from behind us, laughing. "You'll run off all my customers."

Deb looked over her shoulder and smiled, then cut her eyes back to the man. "I'm just kidding," she said with a chuckle. "I just have cancer."

When we turn our trials over to God, he truly does turn our heartache into laughter, even if it means sending a bald woman into a hair-styling salon.

God has brought me laughter, and everyone who hears about this will laugh with me. (Genesis 21:6 NIV)

This story first appeared in *Kisses of Sunshine for Women*, compiled by Carol Kent and Thelma Wells, published by Zondervan in 2005.

Reincarnation or Resurrection?

Two years after I had breast cancer, I went through reconstruction surgery. We'd been told the operation would last six to eight hours, so I told my husband to go to work and I'd see him after the surgery.

When I started to come out from under the anesthesia, I thought I had died and gone to Hell. I was being poked and pushed (excruciating pain) and I couldn't speak (had an endotracheal tube in place). A voice told me to relax and breathe through my nose—that I had just been through seventeen hours of surgery.

Then I knew I must have been reincarnated in someone else's body. My surgery was not supposed to take that long. As I regained full consciousness, I discovered I really HAD been under seventeen hours—there had been problems because my circulatory system was like none the surgeons had seen before. When the general surgeon had done the mastectomy of my right breast prior to the reconstruction, he'd found blood vessels he couldn't identify. And my vessels were smaller than most. When the surgeon had cut the bleeders to look for the feeder vessels, he discovered the ones he'd cut *were* those vessels. The blood vessels involved usually come straight up through the abdominal muscle. Mine did an "S" curve. When I was "knit together in my mother's womb," the Lord must have "purled" too.

I also learned my plastic surgeon was one of only four in the country who could have completed the surgery successfully. I'd not been nervous prior to the surgery, as the Lord had been with me every step of the way in my cancer journey. He'd brought me through my first mastectomy surgery and recovery, and now, he'd brought me through this one. He'd been involved from the start—from our selecting just the right surgeon, to guiding his hands, to bringing me safely through all those extra hours under anesthesia. I felt I had been resurrected.

My husband, expecting to see me in my room, arrived only to be told I was still in surgery. He waited from six p.m. to three thirty a.m. for me to come out of the operating room. He told me later that he'd not been worried, but had felt that "peace that passes all understanding" the entire time. And besides, the nurse had kept coming out to give him progress reports.

One of the bonuses of the long surgery—I was in an extra-care room, and my room was one of the only rooms with good air-conditioning. Baltimore was enduring a tremendous heat wave. I had the best nursing care ever. They all came into my room to cool off!

God is good and cares about all the details in our lives. He promises he'll always be with us and certainly kept his promise with me.

I Will Fear No Evil

Be strong and courageous, do not be afraid or tremble at them, for the LORD your God is the one who goes with you. He will not fail you or forsake you (Deut. 31.6 NASB).

Wincing with each tiny movement, I eased slowly from side to side trying to find a comfortable position. Hours dragged past as sleep eluded me. Earlier that day, I'd been released from the hospital after an arduous surgery that kept me in intermediate care and on medication far longer than anticipated. The medication and my inability to take in more than fruit juices and Italian ices made me terribly weary and weak—if only I could sleep!

Finally, I drifted off into an uneasy sleep. Seemingly seconds later, I awoke—startled! Ants or bugs crawled all over me, trying to get out from under my skin! Writhing all over, I cried. I realized I was coming down from the medicine and sugar high I'd been on for days.

Then the taunter struck. "See what your faith and your God have done now—all that courage and comfort he supposedly is to you? And now he's deserted you just when you need him most! What a testimony you are."

"Go away, Satan! God is here—I know he's still here!"

"Oh, sure he is. And what about sleep and all these crawlies? If he were here, he'd take care of those problems."

Praise songs rang through my mind. The trumpets of battle songs pierced the fog in my brain. Over and over, I repeated the songs and the twenty-third Psalm. "I shall not want … though I walk through the valley of death, I shall fear no evil." A warmth and peace flooded me. I knew without question God was with me, right then. The "itchy-crawlies" eased. The notes and words of the songs chorused a battle lullaby.

Finally, I slept. When morning came, I was rested and refreshed.

Thank you, Lord, for promising you will never leave me or forsake me. Thank you for letting me sleep on your shoulder. You are here with all of us always.

A Godly Woman's Influence

On a Christian Women's Club speaking tour, I was hosted by two delightful Christian women. While there, I picked up a book by Florence Littauer on the Personalities. I was so intrigued by this theory that I tried the "test" out on my husband when I returned home. That's a story in itself!

About a year later, I saw Florence was speaking at a conference in Colorado and decided to attend. Flo's talk so intrigued me with her talk about personalities and speaker training, as did a chance meeting with her daughter Marita, that I asked Roy for the upcoming CLASSeminar as a birthday present.

That seminar was the start of a long and fulfilling relationship with the Littauers and with CLASS. I insisted my husband attend a CLASS to show him why I was so involved, and accidentally ended up on staff when another staffer became ill. When Flo and Marita decided to start the Personality Seminars, I was asked to join them. There, I learned that even a Powerful Choleric can serve in the background when it is important to do so. Over the years, as a part of the team, I learned to not only speak, but more importantly to listen. I thought God had given me this opportunity to make me a better speaker.

Then I got breast cancer, which put a huge damper on all my plans. I couldn't speak to groups—they didn't want a bald woman trying to motivate them. My mother-in-law passed away shortly thereafter, and a year later, our son was killed in a tragic automobile accident. Speaking was not in the cards, but lots and lots of listening was.

I'd attended a Bible study group in our community off and on for several years. Imagine my surprise when I was asked to be the leader. All of my CLASS training came into play along with my memory for "trivia," Bible knowledge, and the listening skills I'd learned. God had been leading me to that appointment for years—through all the training, and all the tragedies. He'd been equipping me for just this role with those women who needed to learn about the wonderful relationship they could have with Jesus. He gave me insights I needed to help them understand the Scriptures we were studying, and I saw several women accept his salvation.

Recently, I had an opportunity to attend the study again as a visitor. The women have grown so much in their walk with the Lord. Several of them are now taking a leadership role.

I remembered what Florence always told the students at the end of each seminar—that during the seminar she (and Marita and I and the other staff) had been their Pauls—training them in the way they should go—and they had been our Timothys. She challenged us to go out and be Paul—and train our own Timothys. This Bible study showed me that I had done just that—and I was blessed to see my own Timothys become Pauls.

God Is in Control

How many times do we rush blindly into our days, perhaps breathing a brief "God guide me" on our way out of the bedroom to get coffee and dive into our plans? I was reminded recently our plans may not be those God has for us.

I was scheduled for a total hip replacement on December 20, 2016. During the pre-op checkup with my general practitioner, they found a change in my EKG from the previous year. Obviously, they weren't going to okay the surgery until they were sure I could handle the operation. So, on December 16, I had a heart catheterization. They discovered my blood vessels had no blockages, but the left ventricle of the heart was enlarged, and the rate of blood being pumped out (ejection fraction) was below normal.

My cardiologist looked at my records and asked, "Do you remember what chemo regimen you had when you were being treated for breast cancer in 2000?

"Yes, I had four cycles of Cytoxin and Adriamycin."

"I thought so," he replied. "You have chemo-induced cardiomyopathy. Your heart has been damaged by the chemo and the effects have shown up now. You are in the beginning stages of congestive heart failure."

One of my friends, upon hearing the diagnosis, quipped, "Of course! You have always had a big heart!"

The surgery was okayed and proceeded as scheduled. I recovered better than expected. At my three-week checkup on January 11, the surgeon told me I was good to go, and he'd see me in a month. Visiting nurses checked me one last time on the 12th and discharged me. All was well in my world, and I was plunging into the work and writing I had planned.

At 4:05 a.m., Friday the 13th, I woke up with a racing heart—really racing! We called 911, and I went by ambulance to the ER. Three hours later, they managed to get my heart back into sinus rhythm. The cardiologist, suspicious of the cause, ordered ultrasounds of my legs and a chest scan. He told us, "Number one, it could be just an isolated event; number two, it's a clot; number three, it's a clot; number four, it's a clot. He was correct; in fact, I had two clots in my upper leg and a pulmonary embolism in my lower right lung. Many blood tests later, I came home on the evening of the January 17.

I tell you all this because I believe God knew what would happen and had me in the palm of his hand. If I hadn't had the EKG anomaly, the cardiologist would not have had the information he needed for his diagnosis. If the atrial fibrillation episode hadn't occurred, we would not have known about the clots. I could have stroked out at any time. I call these occurrences "God-cidences." God knew, he acted, he took care of me through the doctors and nurses and other professionals.

My life verse is James 1:2: "Count it all joy my brothers, when you meet trials of various kinds, for you know that the testing of your faith produces steadfastness. And let steadfastness have its full effect, that you may be perfect and complete, lacking in nothing" (vs 2-4, ESV).

I count it all joy these God-cidences took place to demonstrate to me and others that our God is in control.

So, before you go rushing off into your plans, take time to stop and ask God to show you his plans and then "Count it all joy!"

My Mother's Hands

I looked down today as I was typing and saw my mother's hands—wrinkled, age-spotted, slightly shaky. I looked into my mirror today and saw my mother's face—wrinkled, pale blue eyes, white hair.

But she's not here! my inner child cried. *How can I be seeing her?*

Then I realized I was seeing my hands—I've grown old. I am not as sprightly as once I was. Aches and pains are a normal part of my life. I've slowed down, but time has sped up.

How can that be? Only yesterday, I was riding my bike with my friends and stealing apples off the sheriff's tree. Only yesterday, I was eating shrimp pizza at the Spoon across the street from Macalester. Only yesterday, I smiled at Roy with tears in my eyes as I became his wife. Only yesterday, I cruised the world with Mom on Silversea. Only yesterday, we moved to Orlando in the sun and fun. Only yesterday, Boot Pond became our home. How can seventy-some years have passed when I still feel twelve at times? How can we have been married over thirty-six years? How can that little girl in the fuzzy bear coat be mom to our nine-year-old grandson?

Time is curious. Time passes so slowly when we're anticipating something and races by when we're not looking. And I've become my mom. A needlepoint picture she lovingly crafted for me sums up what I'm saying.

"Mirror, mirror on the wall—I'm my Mother after all!"

MOM

She was gracious and charming
She had a good life.
She brought up a daughter,
She was a good wife.

They worked hard, and played hard,
They always had fun.
Their family, their friends,
They loved every one.

Her husband, my father,
Slept away years ago.
She mourned him, and missed him,
And too wanted to go.

She lived with her daughter,
And a son she held dear;
But her body was tired,
She'd lived many years.
She was soundly asleep;

Her breathing was even.
Between one breath and the next,
She slipped into heaven.

Reunited with Daddy in Heaven above,
Hugging and laughing—enjoying the Lord.
Talking and greeting the ones she had loved,
Rejoicing and praising our wonderful God!

I loved them so dearly,
Parting's sweet pain.
What I've lost on Earth,
Surely is Heaven's gain.

Good memories I have
To hold close in my heart,
One day, I'll be with them,
Never to part.

Grace and peace are my portion,
From my God above
Who walks with my parents,
And sends me their love.

Rest in Peace, Mom.

Starting Over—Again!

Buy a publishing company? At your age? Are you crazy?

I heard all those questions and more in 2016 when I bought a struggling publishing company. I even questioned my sanity myself. Who in the world at age sixty-eight would take over a company in trouble and try to turn around operations to make the business successful?

My mother had come to live with us several years before. During the past few years, she'd been in poor health, and I was her sole caregiver. Her room was on the first floor of our home and our bedroom was upstairs. Because she had been falling frequently, I spent more time and late nights in my downstairs office. A night owl by inclination, I now became a night owl by necessity.

But I couldn't just listen for her. I had to have something productive to do. I wanted to do more than care for her, read, and play computer games. I'd once been a professional speaker giving seminars and teaching at conferences across the US. But breast cancer and a series of family problems took me off the road. I knew, in no uncertain terms, I needed to stay home and care for my family. In the process, I lost myself!

Strange how our identity is often tied up in what we do. No longer a "speaker" or "consultant" or "manager," I couldn't figure out what or who Deb was. Many years and much prayer later, I discovered Deb was just Deb—a unique (some would say weird) individual loved by her family, friends, and God. Just being, just staying at home was fine. And in that, I found peace.

But I wondered why God had gifted me with talents I was no longer using—was his intent to have me waste those gifts? Was this all there was? I was content but curious.

I started an editing service—I'd always edited as I read and had been editing friends' books for free. I figured I'd try to earn some extra money as a freelancer. This was a great activity—I kept busy, was helping others and earning some spending money—and I was home where I could take care of my mom.

Some months later, I met a friend at a writer's conference who told me about her job with a publishing company as the acquisitions editor. She said she was inundated with manuscripts to edit—I offered to help. Two weeks later, she'd hired me as a subcontractor. I spent most of the next year editing some great (and some not-so-great) books. I learned so much about editing from my friend and from going through the process time after time.

When my friend decided to leave the company, the owner asked me to come on board as the Senior Vice President of Acquisitions and Operations. Oh, the seduction of a fancy title! I jumped into the job and worked hard to increase the profitability of my area of responsibility. As time went on, I took over more and more of the operations of publishing as the owner was very ill. Finally, he decided he could no longer run the company, keep up his health, and care for his family.

After much prayer and conversation with my husband, I offered to buy the company. He accepted. My mother had died and I was at a loss for something meaningful to do. So, in my late sixties, I started yet another career. At a time when most folks were retiring, I was starting anew. And I learned God never wastes anything. All the skills and abilities I had gained through the years, along with the gifts he'd given me, were brought into play running the company.

My mission in life now is to come alongside our authors and help them get the words God has given them to the readers who need to see them. My job is to teach and encourage and mentor and guide those authors God gave me—and to acquire new ones. Publishing is not a solitary business—many skill sets are needed to be successful. I have met many people who have caught my vision and are willing to come alongside me and work to fulfill the mission. I get to encourage and teach and mentor and guide them too.

I cannot know what the future will bring—all I can do is stay faithful to the mission I've been given. I've learned you're never "all used up" or "of no use." The time is never too late to start over, to work to help others, and to empower them to be all they can be.

Conclusion

I hope you've enjoyed reading *These Are the Days of My Life* about my personal adventures as much as I enjoyed writing them. As I look back on my life, I think about all of the people who have had an impact on my journey and made everything I've done possible.

One final lesson I've learned, having had joy and sorrow, riches and lack, is I now know the people in our lives with whom we cross paths are the true riches and the ones who bring true joy.

Only with Jesus Christ as my Savior and Lord could I have survived to this point with the hope of a future yet to come. He is the greatest treasure of all.

About the Author

Deb Haggerty is a lover of God, wife, mother, and "Nana." Born in Benson, Minnesota, she graduated from Macalester College, St. Paul, MN, in 1969 with a BA in English Literature and a minor in music and religion.

Deb worked for Southern Bell and AT&T for thirteen years, holding positions from entry level to district level management. While at Southern Bell, she completed an MBA in Human Resources Management and Organizational Design from Mercer University School of Business in Atlanta.

She left AT&T in 1985 to found Positive Connections®, a management consulting and training firm. She worked with organizations that wanted to better communicate with their employees and with individuals who wanted to build better relationships.

After successfully battling breast cancer in 2000, she started a website to encourage others on that path, PositiveHope.com. During the years that followed, Deb served as the Chairman of the Florida Breast Cancer Coalition as well as on the Board of Directors of the National Breast Cancer Coalition.

2010 saw the start of her Christian book review site, PositiveGrace.com. Positive Grace was named one of the top fifty Christian book review sites in 2018.

In 2016, she purchased Elk Lake Publishing, Inc., a Christian publishing company. Deb teaches at many Christian writers' conferences, has been published in over twenty books, and has more than fifty articles to her credit. She loves talking with groups about her relationship with Jesus Christ.

Deb and her husband, Roy, live on beautiful Boot Pond just outside Plymouth, Massachusetts, with Coki the Dog, their adorable miniature dachshund.

She can be found on Facebook as Deb Ogle Haggerty, @ DebHaggerty on Twitter, and DebHaggerty on LinkedIn.

ElkLakePublishingInc.com is her corporate website.

KEYS TO SUCCESSFUL WRITING

Pet Peeves

As an editor, I read—a lot! And I find I get impatient with certain contrivances authors tend to overdo. I realize part of what we do as writers is use our voice, but I also realize part is trying to impress or to ensure our readers get the message or story we're trying to impart. And while our vision is important, we need to remember the best part of reading is employing our imaginations—visualizing the place and time and characters. We need to give our readers the latitude to imagine their own scenes and be drawn in by our words.

One of my prime irritants is over-description. We used to be taught the Rule of Three—use adjectives in trios. This rule is now archaic as readers would rather read action than flowery words. You may choose to use three words, but two are better, and one good word is the best. Over-description leads to telling rather than showing what is happening in the scene. Which is better? "He had sparkling-blue eyes with long eyelashes almost like a girl's." Or, "She adored gazing into his sparkling blue eyes fringed with long dark lashes."

All my authors know two of my pet peeves are the words "it" and "that." I dislike these words because in many cases, they indicate a writer who is taking shortcuts rather than finding a good way to express their sentences. Using "it" often makes a reader pause to try to figure out what "it" represents. Use "it" too often and a reader will get confused, irritated, and quit reading. And that brings me to "that." "That" is an overused word that can often be omitted. (You can often omit the word "that.") See the difference? [I must admit, as I was editing these stories, I too had to delete a raft of thats.]

The best advice I can give a writer is to read their words from their reader's point of view. Did you repeat a phrase or a concept too many times? Readers are smart—you don't need to make a point over and over. Are you using description for description's sake—or to enhance the action? Ensure description adds to the story and doesn't detract from your plot. If in doubt, leave the extra words out! Too much description and readers will skip entire parts of your book or worse—stop reading.

Think of poor Snoopy the writer, "It was a dark and stormy night ..." Instead—"The storm loomed over the pitch black night ..." Your goal is to keep the reader wanting the next words, paragraph, page, and chapter.

I wish you good writing!

The ART of Exceptional Editing

ed•it \\'e-dət\ *vt* [back-formation fr. *editor*] (1791) **1 a : to prepare (as literary material) for publication or public presentation b : to assemble (as a moving picture or tape recording) by cutting and rearranging c : to alter, adapt, or refine esp. to bring about conformity to a standard or to suit a particular purpose.** (*Merriam-Webster's Collegiate Dictionary*, **11th Edition**, p. 396)

Editing is the icing on the book "cake." After the author has labored to produce a manuscript, the editor takes a turn to perfect the manuscript. Obviously, we read the document first. Pre-computer, we'd use a red pencil—making notes of changes to make, areas to tighten up or delete. We'd look for clichés and tired illustrations as well as grammar and punctuation errors. And typos—amazing what ~~misteaks~~ mistakes exhausted fingers can produce!

Today our job is similar, except we labor with Track Changes instead of a red pencil or pen. The computer has made editing both easier and more difficult. Editing is easier as we can make and undo changes with one mouse click instead of writing in the margins or between the lines. We can easily add and delete comments. We can instantly reformat pages or quotes. But using Track Changes has a problem too. Changes are so easy, we can go overboard and erase an author's voice and methodology. We can forget our job: to alter, adapt, or refine

... to suit a particular purpose. We are to assist the author to perfect their work. I communicate with an author frequently while editing. We should work as partners—both striving to improve the quality of the manuscript. When working with experienced authors, that process is completed with little agita or angst. They're familiar with the process and know changes will need to be made. They realize what they've written may be unclear to another reader and need revision. We also meet the "seasoned" authors who believe their work is well-seasoned and resist efforts to perfect the recipe.

New authors are—new. The process is new, Track Changes edits are new, the necessity for proper formatting and following the rules of editing is new. Many new authors are grateful for their editor's help. They know experience can help them perfect their craft and assist them to produce the best possible book. New authors take more of an editor's time because we teach as well as edit ... if we are to meet our responsibilities in preparing their work for publication and to enable enabling the author to write clearer in the future.

The most difficult author is one who thinks they have written a masterpiece, but when we read their work we groan at the banality of the tale. There are typos and grammar and punctuation errors throughout, and the story leaps from point of view to point of view within a single paragraph. When we have to send a manuscript back to be completely rewritten, they don't understand, because "God gave me these words to write!" I've had to relay such bad news to authors—it's never easy.

What can we do to make our (and the authors') jobs less challenging and more collaborative? We can practice the ART of Exceptional Editing. Attention to detail is the A. Make sure the manuscript is grammar, punctuation, and usage errors-free. To accomplish this, we have to stay updated on the latest rules. Reference material (Merriam Webster's Collegiate Dictionary, The Chicago Manual of Style, Webster's Dictionary of Synonyms, the Christian Writer's Manual of Style by Robert Hudson, Proofreading Secrets of Best-Selling Authors by Kathy Ide, and more) should grace our bookshelves and stay current. Rules change; our language is fluid. Old mandatory rules, such as commas surrounding or preceding the word "too" have changed. "But" may no longer need a comma preceding it. The use of the comma depends on the length of the sentence—whether the sentence is short (no comma) or long (comma suggested). Consistency is needed throughout the document. I am grateful when my publishers have a style sheet for the author and me to follow.

The R of ART is Responsiveness. When an author submits their manuscript, they anticipate our prompt response. Is the book good? Do you like it? When do you think you can have changes back to me? To facilitate communication easily, we email back and forth. We should respond to an inquiry or question within twenty-four hours if possible. The burden of responsiveness is upon us. Unless we work efficiently, we delay publication. Once our first pass has gone back to the author, they need to respond expeditiously to accept the changes we've suggested. If they disagree with us, they need to discuss them with us, make any changes of their own, and return the book to us for final edits.

Teamwork brings our ART to fulfillment. When we team up with our authors, we have the best chance of producing a good work. We should practice the "rabbinical method" of editing, "Come, let us sit down together and work to make this perfect" rather than the "Socratic method, "I am the expert. You sit and listen to what I tell you and make the changes I direct you to make." When we function as a team, all the pieces blend and we will enjoy our The ART of Exceptional Editing.

WRITING, TEACHING, ACQUIRING

Eva Marie said to write a post [for the Florida Christian Writers Conference Blog] about writing or about what I'm teaching or about what I'm looking for as an acquisitions editor. Hmm.

Writing. I don't write; I edit. Creativity with words is not my long suit—I'm much better at prettying up other people's words. Oh, I've written some short stories in the past, even some about writing, but do you think I can find them now? Of course not. Did I mention organization is not my strong suit either? I remember some of the titles, though—"Business Suits to Bunny Slippers"—"Those Awful 'D' Words"—"The ART of Exceptional Editing." (I could submit that one, except I think I sent ART in last year.) Hmm.

What I am teaching this year. I'll be teaching networking—the people kind. We'll discuss the pros and cons of the hows and whys to network. We'll learn some rules and even practice. And I'm teaching about some tips and tricks to working with editors and publishers. I've gathered the tips from some of the best in our business, and I'll be sharing them along with what I've learned myself first as a freelancer, then an acquisitions editor, and now a publisher. We'll share our experiences, and I'll share anything about the business you want to know that I know. Hmm.

What I am looking to acquire. First of all, I'm looking for excellent writing—I don't much care about the genre. As long as the writing is excellent, I'll consider publishing the book. Now, mind you, the book must have a Christian focus and not have profane language or descriptive sex scenes. But we publish kid's books, middle-grade books, YA (young adult) books, and adult books—even some for golden agers. We publish romance, historical, mystery, suspense/thriller, science fiction, fantasy, contemporary, and biblical fiction. In other words, if you write an excellent book, we'll find a genre. Of course, if you don't know the audience for whom you're writing, you probably won't sell many books. And then both of us lose. Hmm.

We also publish nonfiction—occasionally. I don't read much nonfiction, and I like to publish what I like to read. So, nonfiction has to hold my attention—has to have a twist, be out of the ordinary. You need to catch my interest quickly and have something new to say. That said, we rarely publish memoirs, devotionals, poetry, or Bible studies (I have contracts out for those for the next five years!). I'm not interested in how you overcame adversity—all of us have—unless there's a good yarn involved. In other words, something that hasn't been done before. Hmm.

And I care tremendously about PUGS as Kathy Ide coined the word. Punctuation, Usage, Grammar, and Spelling are all critical. Over the past year, I can't tell you how many proposals I've rejected because of PUGS. Make sure what you're submitting to an agent or an editor is as perfect as possible. Hmm.

Hmm—I guess that's all for now.

Choose Your Publisher with Care

When an author begins to look at publishers to see where their book might fit, there are several things they should take into consideration. The same steps generally apply to agents as well.

Does the publisher have a good reputation in the industry? With the proliferation of small, boutique publishers popping up constantly, you want to ensure the publisher you choose is honest and has a good image. Unfortunately, even in Christian publishing, there are unethical publishers who only want your money and do not produce a quality product. Investigate carefully.

Has the publisher got a track record? How many books have they published? How many books do they publish in a year? You want to make sure your publisher is not a fly-by-night. They should have published books for a while and have a significant list of books available as well as a variety of authors. Ask for references.

How do they operate? There are a variety of different kinds of publishers. You'll find *pay-to-print* or vanity presses—who'll publish anything as long as you pay them. Some of these presses are legitimate publishers who provide a variety of services for the money, such as EA Book Publishing and Redemption Press. *Hybrid* publishers are a combination of pay-to-print and traditional. You'll need to read their contract carefully (you should read ALL contracts carefully). Some hybrids do not offer any editing—what you send them is what gets printed, errors and all, and they require you purchase a significant number of books. *Traditional* or *royalty* publishers range from large, multi-imprint houses like Tyndale, Broadman/Holman, and Baker Books to small-medium, independent publishers like New Hope, LPC (Lighthouse Publishing of the Carolinas), and Elk Lake Publishing, Inc.

As part of your research and getting to know the requirements for a particular publisher, you may want to ask the following:

- Does the publisher require query letters?
- Proposals?
- Do they accept simultaneous submissions?
- Unagented authors?

Check out the publisher's website for the format required for manuscripts as well as specifications about what they do and don't accept.

What kind of contract does the publisher offer?

- What rights are claimed by the publisher and what rights are left to the author—are rights negotiable?
- If so, which ones?
- How long is the contract period?
- Does the publisher require you to submit new works to them before shopping them to other publishers?
- Can you get out of the contract?
- Can they terminate the contract for any reason before the term is completed?

ALWAYS read everything in the contract carefully.

What genres do they publish?

- Fiction?

- Nonfiction?

- Devotionals?

- Bible Studies?

- Poetry?

- Children's Books?

If Fiction, what areas?

- Romance,

- Historical, Contemporary,

- Mystery/Suspense,

- Fantasy/Science Fiction/Supernatural?

Once you've carefully considered all these items, you'll have a better idea what publishers your book may fit. Be sure when you contact them that everything you submit is pristine from a grammar, punctuation, usage, and spelling standpoint—nothing turns off a prospective publisher (or agent) more than a messy, inaccurate query letter, proposal, or manuscript.

An informed author is smart author—and a good businessperson.

Conference Season Is Upon Us

In the Spring, conference season descends upon us. The advent of this time of the year brings both anticipation and dread to both attendees and faculty alike. Having been an attendee and having served on various faculties, I thought I'd give you some tips from "both sides of the aisle."

Attendees:

- **Be prepared.** Know what the conference is offering. Educational sessions? Meet and greets with faculty, editors, and agents? Retreat time?

- **Bring paperwork** such as lots of business cards and one-sheets, some proposals. A notebook. You'll only need a few proposals as most editors won't want to lug them back home.

- **Be friendly.** Know that everyone there is either outgoing (will probably give you a hug) or introverted (they're so happy you took action first)—don't be afraid to say hello to someone you don't know—you may make their day AND make a new friend.

- **Be considerate.** The person you want to talk with may be on the way to a meeting, a session, or the bathroom. Don't take any abruptness as a brushoff. Try again—perhaps the lunch line or sitting at their table at a meal.

- **Buy books**. The bookstore is a great place to find bargains and get autographed copies of your faves. *You* don't mind the extra weight going home, do you?

Faculty:

- **Be prepared**. Have your presentation materials locked down. Make sure any equipment you have is in good working order. Know your place on the program and the locations you're supposed to be. Get there early.

- **Bring paperwork.** A notebook. Have lots of business cards. Have ample copies of your style sheets, proposal guidelines, and handouts. If your handouts are online, be sure to have the URL and password so attendees can access them.

- **Be friendly**. You're there to meet and greet and talk to the attendees. Yes, I know you may be shy, but step out of your comfort zone. Even a smile may make the day for someone. If you can't talk right then, make an appointment to meet for coffee or just to chat. Let them know you're here for them.

- **Be considerate.** Many attendees have one of two reactions to meeting you—they may be awestruck or terrified they'll look/sound stupid. They have no clue you feel the same way when you run into one of your heroes. Try to smile and give them a few seconds—even if you're in a terrible, "I've got to get there NOW!" rush.

- **Buy books.** The bookstore is a great place to find bargains and get autographed copies of your faves. *You* don't mind the extra weight going home, do you?

Remember—we're all there to learn, to meet people, and to have a good time. Relax, enjoy the setting, take some time for yourself. Look for God appointments and listen. When the conference is over, take time to reflect, pick some keepers from your notes, write thank-you notes, and prepare for the next conference you attend. If you're very fortunate, you may walk away with a proposal or even the offer of a contract.

Dani Pettrey, in her one of her Monday Cuppa Moment's, said about conference attendance, "Focus on being a blessing to others. Instead of worrying about what you are going to do, focus on helping others. Look for the person sitting alone in the corner and join them. Be the smiling face people see when they walk past you. You will come away full of joy and maybe even with a new friend."

May your writing be successful and **count it all joy!**

PEOPLE ARE IMPORTANT!

No matter how busy you are, you must take the time to make the other person feel important.—Mary Kay Ash

In today's work world, managers and supervisors often feel they have way too much work to perform in way too little time. As a result, many times, the "people" things slip so the "work" gets done. It's easy to push a "person" aside to complete the "project" that's been assigned.

However, study after study shows it's "attitude" that's critical in performance. Employees (and managers and supervisors) perform better if they're made to feel important. When you think about it, making people feel important should not be that difficult a task—they ARE important. If not for the people in our companies, the work would not get done. Too often managers look at the "bottom line" without understanding the "people" produce that bottom line.

Managers complain it takes too much time to make employees feel important. That myth could not be further from the truth. Once you get in the habit, the practice becomes invaluable.

Think a minute about what makes you feel important. Chances are it's not a raise or a big speech or a commendation in front of the group, although those make make you feel special. The smile and "good job" during a rough project, the small compliment on work completed, the acknowledgment you're a valuable part of the team—these are the small things that take little time on the part of a manager but make for big changes in an employee's attitude.

Ken Blanchard's classic book, *The One Minute Manager,* is worth another read. The thesis is those small increments of attention make vast differences in performance. Time has proven that his theory and process is correct. The small, unexpected bits of attention are worth their weight in diamonds.

Retention is a continual problem for businesses. Many employees who leave do so because they didn't feel important to the company. Many have voiced feelings like "I was just a small cog." "They never noticed me, they'll never miss me when I'm gone." "The numbers were more important than the people."

Managers and supervisors who don't take the time to make employees feel important, in themselves and to the team, directly affect the bottom line—negatively. Turnover, hiring, and training employees are some of the biggest drains on company funds and profits. The first step in retaining employees is to make sure the company values its people—and lets them know their value.

Jack Welch, former CEO of GE and known as one of the best CEOs in the country, took time daily to hand write notes to employees to encourage them. His model is one that could and should be adopted by businesses large and small. In fact, my husband, Roy, when he was CEO of a large information technology consulting company, signed birthday, anniversary, and Christmas cards to each one of his employees. As Malcom Forbes once stated, "It's always worthwhile to make others aware of their worth."

Communication—Our Most Important asset

Communication. In over thirty-five years of consulting and speaking, I have found most business problems can be traced to communication: miscommunication, lack of communication, misunderstood communication. Most of us think that by talking we are communicating. Talking isn't communicating, though, because each individual listens, learns, and understands in a unique way.

Understanding our own communication style is a necessary requirement before we can hope to understand and communicate with others. Once we know our style of communication, we can begin to learn to modify it to match the style of someone else. For us to ensure communication occurs, we must speak in a manner the other person understands.

Communication is the sum of what we do in an interaction with another—the words we use, our tone of voice, and our body language. Peter Drucker said, "Communication is understanding what is not said." The entire conversation, verbal and nonverbal, must be decoded in order to truly communicate.

The art of communication necessitates knowledge of the mechanics of communication. Webster defines communication as "a process by which information is exchanged through a common system of symbols, signs, or behavior; a technique for expressing ideas effectively." The thesaurus gives several choices of words for communication: interaction, transmission, contact, connection, touch, interchange. Communication requires us to interact, transmit, and connect with the proper message.

If communication is critical, feedback should be sought to ensure the message received was the same as that which was sent. Ask the recipient to repeat back the statement, or rephrase what was said to demonstrate the message was properly received.

Many times "noise" gets in the way of proper communication. Noise refers to any of the distractions that can get in the way of the correct sending or receiving of messages. Anything from actual outside sounds, other people in the area, or the sender's/receiver's own perceptions or moods are noise. Keeping noise from interfering with the intent of the communication is a constant effort.

One of the biggest generators of noise is our personalities. Personality largely dictates how an individual will listen, learn, and understand. In order to communicate well, each of us must discover who we are from a personality standpoint and recognize our communication style is primarily governed by that personality type.

What is personality? Personality is the essence of who we are. That part of us which makes us uniquely who we are is our personality or, as some people refer to it, temperament. Personality is part of our genetic makeup and, as such, is unique to each individual. Oswald Chambers, well-known philosopher-theologian, professes, "Personality is that peculiar, incalculable thing that is meant when we speak of ourselves as distinct from everyone else." Personality is what makes us who we are and why we act and react the way we do.

Studies of identical twins conducted by the University of Minnesota indicate that heredity is responsible for approximately two-thirds of our personality make-up. Our parents and grandparents have passed down to us personality characteristics much as they have eye or hair color. The remaining one-third of our personality is shaped by the environmental effects of birth order, the locale in which we grew up, the kinds of experiences we had in school, college, and work, and any significant or traumatic events in our lives. Personality type, that "incalculable thing," which makes us uniquely us and determines communication style is decided before we are born and honed by life experiences.

The study of personality is not new. The first documented study of personalities was done by Hippocrates, the father of modern medicine, about 400 BC. Hippocrates, wandering around ancient Greece, noticed there were people who had very different styles of acting and talking and being. A curious individual, Hippocrates decided to study the matter and see if a rationale for what caused variations in behavior could be discovered. His hypothesis, after much study, was the differences could be ascribed to the prevalence of various kinds of bodily fluids that coursed through each person's body. He identified four basic types of fluids that influenced a person's behavior. The names of these fluids or "humors" are still utilized by some systems of personality studies today.

SANGUINE

Hippocrates felt those people who were very flamboyant, talked loudly, and gestured widely had a great amount of rich, red blood running through their arteries, so he designated them by the Greek word for blood—*Sanguine*. People who are outgoing, like approval, need to be the center of attention, and love to have fun fit this personality type. The word remains in use today to describe someone who is sturdy and cheerful.

CHOLERIC

Individuals who seemed to be very determined, very work oriented, very much in charge, took control of events and ran things, he called ***Choleric.*** He opined these people had an excess of yellow bile, or *cholera*, prevalent in their systems. Today we refer to people who feel they are always correct and are easily moved to unreasonable or excessive anger when challenged as choleric in nature; i.e. hot-headed or what we know today as the Type A personality.

MELANCHOLY

The third type of personality was that of the sensitive artists and writers, musicians and actors—those people who seemed to really be in touch with the feelings of others, nature, and the world around them. These individuals seemed to have a dual nature, another side to their personalities. They were frequently very organized, very detailed, did well with numbers, and liked precision and order in their lives. The substance Hippocrates felt ruled their bodies was black bile or *melan*. Therefore, he called them ***Melancholy***. Today, people of a sensitive nature who are easily depressed by events surrounding them are called melancholy or "blue."

PHLEGMATIC

The last type of person Hippocrates observed was the ***Phlegmatic***. *Phlegma* or phlegm was one of the four humors in early physiology and was considered to be cold and moist and to cause sluggishness. People with a prevalence of this humor in their systems were quiet, slow-paced, and liked the easygoing, placid life. A word coined to describe this type of personality is "stolid"—a combination of steady and solid.

Studies of personality types have continued to the present day. There are literally hundreds of systems. Perhaps the most well known is the sixteen characteristic Myers-Briggs. Others are the DISC, the Personality Puzzle developed by Florence and Fred Littauer, Dr. Tony Alessandra's Platinum Rule, and the Enneagram, a nine-faceted system.

Discovering your type of personality is easily done by taking one of the tests prevalent on the internet. No matter what the four types (or sixteen or nine) are called, they are all quite similar and derive from Hippocrates work or later that of Karl Jung.

Personality survey systems use different words to describe the same or similar personality styles. We will further develop the styles and words Hippocrates used.

SANGUINE

Another word used for sanguine is *popular* or *expressive* or *socializer*. People who are the center of attention at parties, who like to tell jokes, who like to be around people, and who are very outgoing fit in this category. They love to tell stores, but sometimes, the stories bear very little resemblance to what actually happened or the truth. However, the Sanguine feels if embellishment makes for a better story, that's perfectly acceptable. They tend to gesture widely—huge gestures, lots of gestures—in fact, if you tell a Sanguine not to use their hands to talk, they're practically at a loss for words.

> When I first started working for a large communications company, I had a sales job and was visiting a customer with my manager, Joe. He was not exactly pleased the company had allowed females into sales positons. At this time in the early 1970s, the women's rights era was just beginning. Joe was trying to train me to be the same kind of salesperson he was. He was a very quiet person, very reserved, and my

outgoing style clashed with his. As we were traveling to the customer's premises, he told me I needed to get more serious about my job and I was not to use my hands to make a point while speaking with the client. The worst sales call I have ever been on in my life followed. I could not talk. I was so self-conscious about my hands, I could not seem to find the verbal words I needed to illustrate my points.

A Sanguine loves to be the center of attention. They also communicate non-verbally by the kinds of clothes they wear. They tend to dress in the latest styles or trends. Female Sanguines wear bright colors and interesting fabrics and somewhat fashionable or out-of-the-ordinary combinations of accessories. Males wear bright Polo shirts, pocket handkerchiefs, patterned socks, or flamboyant ties. Sanguines dress to stand out in a crowd.

Although they like to be in the center of a group of people, Sanguines are always looking around to see if there is something more interesting or fun going on elsewhere. Above all curious, they keep an eye out for what's happening. Not that they're not interested in the group they're with—there just might be someone else who needs them a bit more. They are easily distracted, usually jump from one thought to another while talking, and may wander off in mid-sentence. They are also personally affectionate and likely to invade another's personal space.

CHOLERIC

A typical Type-A personality, Cholerics are the *drivers*, the *directors*, the *powerful* people of the world. They are workaholics and can be counted on to get the job done if something needs action. They come to the point very quickly and prefer to get data in bullet points. They are abrupt in style and want you to "cut to the chase" "get to the bottom line." Communication is a distraction. They just want to get to work.

Cholerics use very precise, very abrupt gestures when they want to make a point. In fact, if someone is pointing their finger at you and gesturing, they're probably a Choleric. Because they are so driven by goals, they will do whatever it takes to get the job done. A popular bumper sticker reads "Those of you who think you're always right are very irritating to those of us who are." That sums up a Choleric perfectly, because they are usually right. The drive to get their goals accomplished is so strong they sometimes steamroll over people who get in the way. "The means justifies the end" is sometimes their belief, and they'll manipulate or push or yell or do the work themselves to get their way and get the job done.

In clothing choices, Cholerics are a cross between the Sanguine and the Melancholy. Choleric men may start out in a suit with their red power tie and short-sleeved shirt, but will end up with the suit coat off and tie askew as they dig into whatever work needs to be done. Choleric women favor accents of red as red is perceived as a power color. And power means control—Cholerics are all about control so they can achieve their aims.

MELANCHOLY

The Melancholy is almost the direct opposite of the Sanguine. The Sanguine is loud; Melancholies are quiet. Sanguines gesture wildly; Melancholies use very few gestures and keep them close to the body and precise. They speak in an orderly, logical fashion, and, in fact, *logical* is one of the words commonly use to describe them. Having things in order, being perfect, is the driving force for a Melancholy. They carefully consider their words before speaking and require large amounts of data before making a decision. They will talk and talk until they are sure you have been presented the entire picture they wanted you to hear. A Sanguine, on the other hand, will talk just to hear themselves.

Melancholies are easy to recognize from their clothing and demeanor. They dress in subdued, classic styles because they want to look perfect at all times to convey their perfect, orderly, organized image. Clothing purchases are of high quality that will not go out of style in muted colors of gray, navy, and black. They are the pressed and spit-polished people.

Very much into charts and graphs, Melancholies like to have back-up data, detailed information, and precise methodologies to show you what it is that they are trying to communicate. This overload of information can be very irritating to others—especially Cholerics.

Because part of their personality is very sensitive, they tend to reflect the moods of folks around them. Their moods are balanced. If they're depressed, they may be pensive, quiet, and withdrawn as opposed to the Sanguine, who, when depressed, lets the world know.

Many Melancholies are great artists, musicians, actors, and authors because they wish to communicate the beauty, wonder, or emotion of what they see and feel around them to the rest of the world. Their ability to think about and observe what goes on around them aids them in that task.

But also, because they are so sensitive, they've been known to hold a grudge for years. However, proper groveling and apologies will bring a smile back to their faces if they sense you are sincere.

PHLEGMATIC

The final personality type in this system is the Phlegmatic. Easygoing and relaxed describes them. They do not like conflict, so they are the *mediators*, *peaceful* ones, the *relaters*. People who, faced with conflict, loud voices, and apparent anger, will attempt to calm the situation down. They are very good at diplomacy, at listening to others' points of view.

Phlegmatics are nice people, the kind you like to have as friends, as they are extremely loyal. In a gathering, they are probably on the edges—not going out of their way to start conversations but willing to talk if you come to them. The most laid back of all the personalities, their speech is a bit slower. They have a superbly dry sense of humor, and their tongue-in-cheek quips will take you unawares. The response is usually a "Oh, no! I should have seen that coming." Said result amuses them no end.

Reflecting their relaxed being, their clothing follows suit, one item they won't wear unless forced to do so. A sport coat and khakis is more their dress-up style. They'll always dress appropriately but in the most casual clothes acceptable for the occasion.

Phlegmatics are good workers, steady and reliable. They continue to work despite chaos around them. However, if they're given a task they don't want to do, they're masters of procrastination. "Oh! You meant you wanted this today?" They work well in a variety of positions especially those where tact and diplomacy are required. Some of our best diplomats have been Phlegmatics because of their ability to see both sides of a question and mediate an amiable solution for all concerned.

While there are four distinct personality types in this system, most people are a blend of two. My husband, Roy, is an off-the-charts Choleric with just enough Melancholy to drive me crazy. He can unerringly ask the one question I don't have an answer to. Numbers seem to talk to him. He has enough of the Melancholy to process information carefully before making a decision, as opposed to the pure Choleric who makes snap decisions.

I'm a blend of Choleric and Sanguine. Where I may be task-oriented and focused on getting the job done, I also make quick decisions. I like to talk with people and, given a choice, wear bright colors/patterns in my clothing. The Sanguine in me also wants approval, applause for what I'm doing, as well as my Choleric need for praise for a job well done.

Because Roy and I are both Cholerics, occasionally there are conflicts. We have learned over almost forty years to determine whether the issue is worth fighting over or if there is conflict because of our need to be right and in control. Once clarified in our minds, we communicate quite well.

Communication is critical. A recognition of the various personality types and their preferred methods of communicating is imperative if we're to work together successfully. Knowing the types allow us to understand the styles of others and how insisting on our personal styles can negatively impact communication.

How can we understand who we are, our style of communication, then take that a step further and truly communicate with others whose styles are different?

Tony Alessandra, PhD, author of *The Platinum Rule*, espouses a very relevant theory of communication. Most of us grew up with the Golden Rule: "Do unto others as you would have them do unto you." Tony teaches us to go deeper and to practice the Platinum Rule: "Do unto others as they would have you do unto them." In other words, if we truly want to communicate, to translate, to facilitate communication—to interact, transmit, and connect with the proper message—we need to discover the needs of others and their preferred style of speech. Once we understand communication comes from the inside out, we can moderate our behavior so our conversation is on an equal level with someone else's style—not out of our own personality.

Go forth, hold intelligent and thoughtful conversations, and remember to "Count it all joy!"

Made in the USA
Monee, IL
29 January 2020